I Have a Dream

I Have a Dream

Martin Luther King Jr. and the Future of Multicultural America

Edited by James Echols

Fortress Press
Minneapolis

I HAVE A DREAM
Martin Luther King Jr. and the Future of Multicultural America

Cover photo © Flip Shulke/Corbis. Used by permission.
Cover design: Brad Norr Design
Interior design: Beth Wright

Scripture quotations from the New Revised Standard Version Bible, copyright ©
1989 by the Division of Christian Education of the National Council of the
Churches of Christ in the USA, are used by permission.

Scripture taken from the *Holy Bible, New International Version*, copyright © 1973,
1978, 1984 International Bible Society, is used by permission of Zondervan Pub-
lishing House. All rights reserved.

ISBN 0-8006-3685-6

The paper used in this publication meets the minimum requirements of American National Standard for Information Sciences — Permanence of Paper for
Printed Library Materials, ANSI Z329.48-1984.

Manufactured in the U.S.A.
08   07   06   05   04   1   2   3   4   5   6   7   8   9   10

Contents

About the Contributors

James Echols is President of the Lutheran School of Theology at Chicago.

James A. Forbes Jr. is Senior Minister of the Riverside Church, New York City, and formerly Joe R. Engle Professor of Preaching at Union Theological Seminary in New York City. He is the author of *The Holy Spirit and Preaching* (1989).

Robert M. Franklin is Presidential Distinguished Professor of Social Ethics at Emory University's Candler School of Theology. He is author of, among other titles, *Another Day's Journey: Black Churches Confronting the American Crisis* (Fortress Press, 1997) and *Liberating Visions: Human Fulfillment and Social Justice in African-American Thought* (Fortress Press, 1990).

Justo L. González was recently Visiting Professor of Church History at Columbia Theological Seminary, Decatur, Georgia. Among his numerous works are *The Changing Shape of Church History* (2002) and *For the Healing of the Nations: The Book of Revelation in an Age of Cultural Conflict* (1999).

Dwight N. Hopkins is Professor of Theology at the University of Chicago Divinity School and author or editor of many works, including *Down, Up, and Over: Slave Religion and Black Theology* (Fortress Press, 2000) and *Heart and Head: Black Theology—Past, Present, and Future* (2002).

Emilie M. Townes is Carolyn Williams Beaird Professor of Christian Ethics at Union Theological Seminary, New York City. She is author and editor of many works, including *Breaking the Fine Rain of Death: African American Health Issues and a Womanist Ethic of Care* (1998) and *Embracing the Spirit: Womanist Perspectives on Hope, Salvation, and Transformation* (1997).

Peter J. Paris is Elmer G. Homrighausen Professor of Social Ethics at Princeton Theological Seminary. Among his many works are *The Spirituality of African Peoples: The Search for a Common Moral Discourse* (Fortress Press, 1995) and *Black Religious Leaders: Conflict in Unity* (1991).

Linda E. Thomas is Professor of Theology and Anthropology at the Lutheran School of Theology at Chicago. She is the editor of *Living Stones in the Household of God: The Legacy and Future of Black Theology* (Fortress Press, 2003) and author of *Under the Canopy: Ritual Process and Spiritual Resilience in South Africa* (1999).

Introduction

James Echols

———

I will never forget a trip I took as a teenager with my family to visit relatives in Atlanta. On the date of our departure, as my adult cousin was escorting us to an airport gate, she stopped abruptly and asked an African American man coming in the other direction to greet her cousins. At that point, this individual for whom she worked at the Southern Christian Leadership Conference, Martin Luther King Jr., came over, shook our hands, and said a few words before continuing on his way. What a thrill it was to touch the dreamer. In this volume, we all do.

In a 1961 commencement address at Lincoln University, Dr. King declared that "America is essentially a dream." Thus, his historic "I Have a Dream" speech, delivered two years later, both extended and intended to expand the American tradition of dreaming. On one level, it implicitly extended a tradition that includes the seventeenth-century Puritan dream of freedom from religious persecution, the eighteenth-century colonists' dream of political independence, and the nineteenth-century immigrants' dream of economic opportunity. For the vast majority of Americans, religious freedom, political independence, and economic opportunity have constituted central aspects of the "American dream."

On another level, the speech explicitly intended to expand the American tradition of dreaming in the twentieth century by calling all Americans fully to embrace and include racial and ethnic equality as a key aspect of the American dream. Delivered just nine years after the United States Supreme Court *Brown versus Board of Education* decision, Dr. King articulated his dream in light of the nightmare of racism, asserting that this nation's legacy of slavery, segregation, and discrimination involving people of African descent had to be challenged and overcome. And while the Civil Rights Act of 1964 and the Voting Rights Act of 1965 made significant legal strides toward fulfilling the dream, Dr. King died five years later knowing that the nightmare still persisted.

Thirty years after Dr. King's "I Have a Dream" speech, two scholars confirmed the continuing persistence of the nightmare. In *Two Nations: Black and White, Separate, Hostile, Unequal*, Dr. Andrew Hacker stated unequivocally that the "fact remains that most white people believe that, compared with other races, persons of African ancestries are more likely to carry primitive traits in their genes. Given this premise—and prejudice—the presumption follows that most individuals of African heritage will lack the intellectual and organizational capacities the modern world requires." Similarly in *Race Matters*, Dr. Cornel West wrote that "white America has been historically weak-willed in ensuring racial justice and has continued to resist fully accepting the humanity of blacks."

The contributions to this volume were prepared by a distinguished group of scholars and theologians for the 2003 Hein-Fry Lecture Series of the Evangelical Lutheran Church in America both to observe the fortieth anniversary of Dr. King's "I Have a Dream" speech and to explore its implications for the future of America.

In 1963 Dr. King's speech assumed a bicultural society in which issues related to racial and ethnic justice primarily needed to be resolved between people of African and European descent. At the beginning of the twenty-first century, America has become a multicultural society in which people of Native American, Hispanic/Latino, African, Asian, and Arab descent will soon outnumber people of European descent. Just so, the "I Have a Dream" speech must be modified and expanded to incorporate the diversity of God's humanity.

As you read and reflect on this volume, you will discover that some of the writers examine the speech itself, while others explore the larger social context. Several themes are woven throughout all the chapters and knit them together. One theme focuses on Martin Luther King Jr. in terms of both his upbringing and the formative influences that contributed to his ministry. A second theme concentrates on the speech itself, providing analysis, insight, and wisdom into its various political and religious sources. A third theme explores this nation's contemporary twenty-first century social and multicultural cultural setting and the continuing relevance and importance of Dr. King's dream. And finally, a fourth theme emphasizes the divine call to all of God's people to participate in the ongoing struggle for human equality and human justice.

When I became president of the Lutheran School of Theology at Chicago in 1997, my predecessor presented me with a gift that I continue to cherish. On the wall of my office is a photograph of the Rev. Dr. Martin Luther King Jr. making an address, wearing a light tie and a dark suit, his left hand resting on a mound of materials on a podium. And inscribed on the picture are the words, "I Have a Dream," words that recall Dr. King's magnificent speech delivered August 28, 1963, on the steps of the Lincoln Memorial as a part of the March on Washington, one of the mountaintop events of the Civil Rights Movement.

All of us have been touched by Dr. King's ministry in general and his "I Have a Dream" speech in particular. May this volume remind you of the dream and challenge you to work, in creative ways, for a multicultural America that honors and respects the full and equal humanity of God's diverse human family.

chapter 1

King's Vision of America
An Ethical Assessment

Peter J. Paris

—◄

In celebration of the fortieth anniversary of Dr. Martin Luther King Jr.'s "I Have a Dream" speech, this volume demonstrates the enduring significance of his words as the clearest societal vision ever portrayed of what America can and should be. If America is to be a racially just nation, King's vision must be normative for every political platform and public policy agenda throughout the nation. This particular chapter will describe the context of the March on Washington, analyze the structure of his speech, remind you of its content, and evaluate its ethical import.[1]

During his short lifetime Martin Luther King Jr. became a world citizen. Out of the segregated crucible of Atlanta's black ghetto, a young man emerged into the public realm of national and international visibility—a man destined to lead his people and nation out of the bitter experience of racial oppression into a new era of freedom and justice. Reluctantly, he accepted the ominous responsibility that had been thrust upon him. For little more than a decade thereafter he saturated the nation's public arenas with thousands of speeches and sermons aimed at clarifying the nature of the moral problem that threatened to destroy the social order. In those many prophetic utterances he sought to justify his opposition to racism by appealing to the principles in the nation's founding documents, and to the biblical symbols of love and justice long revered in his black church tradition. Thus, rising from a social biography of low esteem, Martin Luther King's name became a household term on six continents by the time he was thirty years old. The incremental victories he achieved from 1956 onward culminated in the 1963 March on Washington, where Dr. King delivered his most memorable "I Have a Dream" speech.

On that historic occasion, the eyes and ears of African peoples everywhere were focused on this young African American man whose public speeches and deeds were being celebrated by a quarter-million people gathered at the base of the Lincoln Memorial in Washington D.C. In his opening sentence King described the occasion as one that "will go down in history as the greatest demonstration for freedom in the history of our nation."

King's speech was crafted for all who had ears to hear. It was a declaration proclaimed to America on behalf of all African peoples. His speech was grounded in the collective memory of his listeners, the second sentence of which vividly evoked that remembrance. "Fivescore years ago, a great American, in whose symbolic shadow we stand today, signed the Emancipation Proclamation." That act liberated from slavery all peoples of African descent whose ancestors had been snatched from their homeland and forced to endure bondage either here or elsewhere for nearly three centuries. Reflecting on that event, King described the decree as "a beacon light of hope to millions of Negro slaves who had been seared in the flames of withering injustice." Summing up its meaning, King eloquently declared, "It came as a joyous daybreak to end the long night of their captivity."

Quickly moving from the past to the present, Dr. King boldly and clearly announced the charge that the Civil Rights Movement had leveled against the United States, namely, that the nation's support for the enduring problem of racial injustice was manifested in the forms of segregation, discrimination, poverty, and domestic exile. That charge could not have been stated more clearly than this:

> But one hundred years later, the Negro still is not free. One hundred years later, the life of the Negro is still sadly crippled by the manacles of segregation and the chains of discrimination. One hundred years later, the Negro lives on a lonely

island of poverty in the midst of a vast ocean of material prosperity. One hundred years later, the Negro is still languished in the corners of American society and finds himself an exile in his own land.

After issuing the indictment, King described the mission of the march thus: "So we've come here today to dramatize a shameful condition." More specifically, he explained the mission by using a metaphor that every American could readily understand. "We've come here to our nation's capital to cash a check." For those who might not know the significance of the check metaphor, Dr. King reminded them:

> When the architects of our republic wrote the magnificent words of the Constitution and the Declaration of Independence, they were signing a promissory note to which every American was to fall heir. This note was the promise that all men, yes, black men as well as white men, would be guaranteed the unalienable rights of life, liberty, and the pursuit of happiness.

Dr. King then abruptly concluded his analysis by saying, "It is obvious today that America has defaulted on this promissory note, insofar as her citizens of color are concerned. Instead of honoring this sacred obligation, America has given the Negro people a bad check, a check which has come back marked 'insufficient funds.'"

But King's response to this announcement is not one of acceptance but an immediate protest: "We refuse to believe that there are insufficient funds in the great vaults of opportunity of this nation." King then restated the mission: "And so we've come to cash this check, a check that will give us upon demand the riches of freedom and the security of justice."

To impress on America the importance of that mission, Dr. King solemnly declared: "We have also come to this hallowed spot"—a spot, I might add, that had been made sacred by the symbol of the great emancipator—"to remind America of the fierce urgency of Now. This is no time to engage in the luxury of cooling off or to take the tranquilizing drug of gradualism." Once again he seized the format of rhetorical repetition by declaring the time for harvesting the coming of a new day:

> Now is the time to make real the promises of democracy. Now is the time to rise from the dark and desolate valley of segregation to the sunlit path of racial justice. Now is the time to lift our nation from the quicksands of racial injustice to the solid rock of brotherhood. Now is the time to make justice a reality for all of God's children.

But if the nation should persist in refusing to honor its promise, Dr. King reminded America of the dire consequences: "It would be fatal for the nation to overlook the urgency of the moment." Why would it be fatal? King's response is simple: "This sweltering summer of the Negro's legitimate discontent will not pass until there is an invigorating autumn of freedom and equality." He elaborated further:

> Nineteen sixty-three is not an end but a beginning. Those who hope that the Negro needed to blow off steam and will now be content will have a rude awakening if the nation returns to business as usual. There will be neither rest nor tranquility in America until the Negro is granted his citizenship rights. The whirlwinds of revolt will continue to shake the foundations of our nation until the bright day of justice emerges.

Dare we consider Dr. King's statement of these consequences as predictive of the so-called "long hot summers" that were destined to engulf many of the nation's cities from 1965 onward?

Then, characteristically, Dr. King spoke directly to his own people by issuing a moral appeal. Fully aware of their moral agency in this great crusade, he was also aware of the temptation to forsake that moral high road in favor of the lowlands of hatred and revenge. And so he admonished them accordingly:

> But there is something that I must say to my people who stand on the warm threshold which leads into the palace of

justice. In the process of gaining our rightful place we must not be guilty of wrongful deeds. Let us not seek to satisfy our thirst for freedom by drinking from the cup of bitterness and hatred. We must ever conduct our struggle on the high plane of dignity and discipline. We must not allow our creative protest to degenerate into physical violence. Again and again we must rise to the majestic heights of meeting physical force with soul force.

In praising the new militancy of the black community, King then reminded all who had gathered that his vision for America was that of an inclusive community in which blacks and whites live in harmony with one another.

The marvelous new militancy which has engulfed the Negro community must not lead us to a distrust of all white people, for many of our white brothers, as evidenced by their presence here today, have come to realize that their destiny is tied up with our destiny. And they have come to realize that their freedom is inextricably bound to our freedom. We cannot walk alone.

But how shall we walk? King immediately focused the crowd's attention on that verb "walk." "And as we walk, we must make the pledge that we shall always march ahead. We cannot turn back."

But even as he encouraged the forward movement, Dr. King was mindful of those who were asking, "When will you be satisfied?" That question prompted an immediate rhetorical rhapsody on the hindrances to our goal.

We can never be satisfied as long as the Negro is the victim of the unspeakable horrors of police brutality. We can never be satisfied as long as our bodies, heavy with the fatigue of travel, cannot gain lodging in the motels of the highways and the hotels of the cities. We cannot be satisfied as long as a Negro in Mississippi cannot vote and a Negro in New York believes he has nothing for which to vote. No, we cannot be satisfied, and we will not be satisfied until justice rolls down like waters and righteousness like a mighty stream.

Thus, the evils of police brutality, discrimination, segregation, indignity, disenfranchisement, hopelessness, and injustice must be overcome.

Dr. King then addressed directly the struggles and sufferings from which the marchers had come to Washington.

> I am not unmindful that some of you have come here out of great trials and tribulations. Some of you have come fresh from narrow jail cells. Some of you have come from areas where your quest for freedom left you battered by the storms of persecution and staggered by the winds of police brutality. You have been the veterans of creative suffering. Continue to work with the faith that unearned suffering is redemptive.

This last phrase is what gives most of my students the greatest problem, namely, "the faith that unearned suffering is redemptive." I say to them what I say to you today: Please note that the suffering King is discussing is the suffering that attends a righteous cause, the quest for freedom. King praised those who suffer in the struggle for justice. He did not praise those who merely suffer abuse in a passive way. That would have been pathological. Rather, he praised the type of suffering undergone by those who work for social transformation. That type of suffering is made redemptive by virtue of the goal it seeks.

Having articulated the nature of the enduring problem of racial discrimination and segregation, having specified the reason for coming to Washington, having warned America of the dire consequences of refusing to grant the rightful claims of its citizens, and having admonished his people and their allies not to substitute violence for the morality of soul force, Dr. King issued the challenge of hope to his listeners as he sent them forth to continue their good work: "Go back to Mississippi; go back to Alabama; go back to South Carolina; go back to Georgia; go back to Louisiana; go back to the slums and ghettos of the northern cities, knowing that somehow this situation can, and will be changed. Let us not wallow in the valley of despair."

Dr. King then described the substance of his hope. Framed in the language of the American dream, King was able to declare that it was deeply rooted in that American dream. Yet unlike the American dream, the novelty of King's vision of America did not lie in a past accomplishment but in a future hope. Dr. King's dream inspired hope in the continuing struggle to realize that desired goal. Thus, in lyrical prose, he described the content of his vision:

And so even though we face the difficulties of today and tomorrow, I still have a dream. It is a dream deeply rooted in the American dream.

I have a dream that one day this nation will rise up and live out the true meaning of its creed: We hold these truths to be self-evident, that all men are created equal.

I have a dream that one day on the red hills of Georgia the sons of former slaves and the sons of former slave owners will be able to sit down together at the table of brotherhood.

I have a dream that one day even the state of Mississippi, a state sweltering with the heat of injustice, sweltering with the heat of oppression, will be transformed into an oasis of freedom and justice.

I have a dream that my four little children will one day live in a nation where they will not be judged by the color of their skin but by the content of their character. I have a *dream* today!

I have a dream that one day, down in Alabama, with its vicious racists, with its governor having his lips dripping with the words of interposition and nullification; one day right down in Alabama, little black boys and black girls will be able to join hands with little white boys and white girls as sisters and brothers. I have a *dream* today!

I have a dream that one day every valley shall be exalted, and every hill and mountain shall be made low, the rough places will be made plain, and the crooked places will be made straight, and the glory of the Lord shall be revealed and all flesh shall see it together.

This is our hope. This is the faith that I go back to the South with.

8   Peter J. Paris

Focusing on the term "faith," Dr. King quickly described its efficacy for the struggle that lay ahead.

> With this faith we will be able to hew out of the mountain of despair a stone of hope. With this faith we will be able to transform the jangling discords of our nation into a beautiful symphony of brotherhood. With this faith we will be able to work together, to pray together, to struggle together, to go to jail together, to stand up for freedom together, knowing that we will be free one day. And this will be the day, this will be the day when all of God's children will be able to sing with new meaning, "My country 'tis of thee, sweet land of liberty, of thee I sing. Land where my fathers died, land of the Pilgrims' pride; from every mountainside, let freedom ring!" And if America is to be a great nation, this must become true.

King's lyrical prose became more and more poetic as he praised the goal of the movement, freedom:

> So let freedom ring—from the prodigious hilltops of New Hampshire.
> Let freedom ring—from the mighty mountains of New York.
> Let freedom ring—from the heightening Alleghenies of Pennsylvania.
> Let freedom ring—from the snow-capped Rockies of Colorado.
> Let freedom ring—from the curvaceous slopes of California.
> But not only that.
> Let freedom ring—from Stone Mountain in Georgia.
> Let freedom ring—from Lookout Mountain of Tennessee.
> Let freedom ring—from every hill and molehill of Mississippi, from every mountainside, let freedom ring!
> And when this happens, when we allow freedom to ring, when we let it ring from every village and every hamlet, from every state and every city, we will be able to speed up that day when *all* of God's children, black men and white men, Jews and Gentiles, Protestants and Catholics, will be able to join hands and sing in the words of the old Negro spiritual, "Free at last, free at last. Thank *God* Almighty, we are free at last."

King's "I Have a Dream" speech was a fitting celebratory culmination to the Civil Rights Movement up to that point. The speech vividly stated the problem, grounded it in the nation's history of slavery and emancipation, demonstrated the nation's betrayal of its promise, and prophesied continued unrest, protest, and the nation's death if it failed to grant African Americans their rightful due. The center of the speech comprised King's vision of America made whole by the fulfillment of its promise: when race will no longer constitute a wall of division within the body politic. Let us hasten to note, however, that he did not proclaim a raceless society. Rather, he described a time when racial differences would have no negative consequences due to the prevalence of harmony and goodwill. That vision seemed worthy of a litany of hope and faith followed by a poetic celebration of freedom.

Since King's assassination his words and deeds have passed from history into the domain of myth and legend. His words have gained immortality and are constantly quoted as moral authority for numerous causes. Virtually every protest against war from that time up to our present day has evoked his words and deeds of non-violent resistance. Ironically, even those whose motives and programs self-consciously contradict King's mission often appeal to his words by shifting their context.

King's societal vision portrays what America can and should become more adequately than does any other speech or document in the nation's history, including the Constitution and the Declaration of Independence. All those who call for a moratorium on the airing of this speech fail to see the relation between political vision, political strategies, and public policies. An adequate societal vision must necessarily precede all non-racist public practices. Such alternative societal visions as those proposed by the ideologies of traditional liberalism, black nationalism, Marxian socialism, laissez-faire capitalism, or communism have failed to offer a constructive solution to the single most enduring problem in the nation's history: racial injustice.

Dr. King creatively synthesized the moral and political and religious insights gained from the social gospel Christianity of his own black church tradition, the democratic ethos implicit in the nation's founding documents, and Mohandas K. Gandhi's philosophy of nonviolent resistance. King's "I Have a Dream" speech eloquently and compellingly revealed his grand, majestic synthesis of all the necessary elements for the most appropriate societal vision ever constructed for this nation. That vision has inspired countless millions of oppressed peoples around the world. That vision laid the groundwork for all subsequent movements of oppressed peoples for liberation and freedom, not only in the political realm but in all phases of their respective lives including economics, culture, religion, education, and others. Among the movements that were influenced directly by Dr. King's thought and practice we can name the following:

- The Black Power movement in this country and among African peoples everywhere, especially in Canada, the Caribbean, and South Africa
- Women's liberation movements among white women and women of color everywhere
- Renewed motivation in various Native American movements
- The migrant farm workers' movement
- The gay and lesbian liberation movement

Dr. King's "I Have a Dream" speech gave America the opportunity for its finest moment in history. But, alas, rather than seizing that moment to usher in a new era in human relations, the nation provided the context for a massive backlash as seen in a number of tragic events: the bombing of Birmingham's Sixteenth Street Baptist Church that killed four little girls at Sunday school a few weeks later; the assassinations of John F. Kennedy, Malcolm X, Medgar Evers, King himself, and Robert F. Kennedy. Just a year following the 1963 March on Washington, President Johnson acknowledged his having given away the Democratic Party in the South to the Republicans by signing the Civil Rights Act of 1964 and the Voting Rights Bill of 1965. Signs of that prediction were seen as early as the 1964 Barry Goldwater campaign, which contained no civil rights plank in its platform; in 1968 President Nixon announced his southern strategy, which was aimed to win the Dixiecrats over to the Republican Party; President Reagan's policy of benign neglect was superseded by President George Bush senior, who used the image of Willie Horton (a recently paroled black male rapist) as a central aspect in his campaign, coupled with the unimaginably insidious act of appointing Clarence Thomas as the replacement for Thurgood Marshall on the Supreme Court; President Bush junior, who window-dresses his cabinet with three blacks while setting himself in opposition to them by vigorously opposing affirmative action—the one program that has helped to correct some of the racial injustices of the past.

Today a disproportionate number of African Americans live in abject poverty, languish in prisons, sit on death row, and suffer from the infection of HIV/AIDS. These are also victims of poor health, high mortality rates, environmental pollution, low educational achievement, and high levels of unemployment. Sociologists view these conditions as the marks of a permanent underclass in the United States.

Clearly America was not ready for such a person as Martin Luther King Jr. America was not ready to hear his message of racial justice. America was not ready to use its vast resources to effect a lasting cure for its racist malignancy that continues to threaten the lives of millions both at home and abroad. Now it is our task to help America to keep alive the societal vision of Martin Luther King Jr. and to work for its full actualization in our time. That vision of America, enunciated so movingly at the base of the Lincoln Memorial on that hot August day in 1963, calls the nation to address the unfinished work and the vast injustices of two centuries of the American republic.

chapter 2

The Poor People's Campaign of 1968
King's Dream Unfulfilled or Unfinished?

Linda E. Thomas

———

Dr. Martin Luther King Jr. delivered the "I Have a Dream" speech on August 28, 1963, at the famous March on Washington. In the United States, we celebrate King's birthday as a national holiday on the third Monday of January. Thousands of people march in cities across the country to remember King's prophetic voice and to continue the work of justice and reconciliation he began. Over forty years have passed since King delivered his landmark speech, but each year it plays over loudspeakers to an ever-changing audience. The celebrations and activism bring together a striking level of multicultural and multigenerational diversity. The public gatherings remind us that King's call to action inspires not only the generation that stood with King, but also each generation since. The rare variety of persons and depth of commitment to King's work has convinced me that the prophetic "Dream" speech has become the most famous and most influential speech in recent United States history.

Let us now seek insight into King's person and prophecy in three ways: first by locating him within the historical stream of prophet-dreamers, second by examining the Poor People's Campaign (PPC) as an important component of King's dream, and finally by reflecting theologically about the timeless prophetic call for God's people to care for persons living in poverty throughout the world.

King as Prophet and Dreamer

Edgar Allan Poe's poem "The Raven" gives a dramatic description of a dreamer:

> Deep into that darkness peering, long I stood there,
>   wondering, fearing,
> Doubting, dreaming dreams no mortal ever dared to
>   dream before.[1]

Mortals we are, and dreamers we are encouraged to be. But to what end? Poe's poetic wanderings echo an even more ancient and universal imaging found in the classic Hebrew Scriptures.

> Now Joseph had a dream. . . . [He said to his brothers] "behold, we were binding sheaves in the field, and lo, my sheaf arose and stood upright; and behold your sheaves gathered around it, and bowed down to my sheaf." His brothers said to him, "Are you indeed to reign over us? Or are you indeed to have dominion over us?" So they hated him yet more for his dreams and his words. . . .
>
> Now his brothers went to pasture their father's flock near Shechem. And his father said to Joseph, "Are not your brothers pasturing the flock at Shechem? Come, I will send you to them. . . . Go now, see if it is well with your brothers and with the flock; and bring me word again. . . . So Joseph went after his brothers, and found them. . . . They saw him afar off. . . . They said to one another, "Here comes this dreamer. Come now, let us kill him." (Gen. 37:5ff. NIV)

The writer of Genesis describes beautifully the relationship between Joseph and his brothers. Joseph was destined to play a special role in God's history. Yet when he shared his dream with his brothers, they responded with outrage and condemnation. Mortals we are and dreamers we are encouraged to be, but to what end?

Like Joseph, the prophets in the Hebrew Scriptures were sometimes dreamers. Indeed, they proclaimed God's word and truth. It is a rare moment when forces in history press together to create an emergent leader who both dreams divine dreams and proclaims

God's truth. Such persons are of a holy substance; we may call them "persons for all seasons." Dr. Martin Luther King Jr. was such a person. He spoke as a prophet to the immediate issues of the 1960s; however, the essence of his message resembles both ancient and postmodern prophetic concerns. King's message belongs to the many strands of prophecy that began outside the land of milk and honey.

King spoke prophetic words, but also he modeled "faith in action." He linked the unambiguous biblical witness of God's love and affection for the poor with God's expectation that the covenant community take responsibility to provide faithfully for and defend the poor.[2] In other words, King's prophetic voice bespoke God's intolerance of structural poverty in a world filled with enough resources for all creation. King's "faith in action" is especially evident in his Poor People's Campaign.

The book of Isaiah provides a source for reflection upon Dr. Martin Luther King Jr. as a prophet. In chapter 62, verse 1, the prophet proclaims boldly that the coming day of salvation for Zion will be signaled by it receiving a new name. The prophet declares, "I will not keep silent . . . I will not rest" until that day comes, until Zion is given a new name by God—a name revealing that a transformation has taken place between God and the people of Zion.

Martin Luther King Jr., like Isaiah of long ago, also cried out, "I will not be silent." King was the grandson of a sharecropper and the son of a Baptist minister. Growing up in America's South exposed King at a tender age to the Jim Crow system of segregation. King deeply desired to bring justice to black people living under unjust Jim Crow laws and decided to become a lawyer. However, he changed his mind after attending Morehouse College. There he learned that a prophetic ministry could and should wrestle with issues like racial segregation, poverty, and political challenges.

Subsequently, King attended Crozer Seminary and after graduation became the pastor of a church in Montgomery, Alabama. On December 1, 1955, something happened in Montgomery that changed King's life. A black woman, Rosa Parks, taking a bus home from work, was seated just behind the "white section." By law, whites sat up front, blacks in the back. Several white people got on the bus. There were no more seats for them in the "white section," so the bus driver ordered Mrs. Parks and three other African Americans to give up their seats. The three others obeyed the driver. Mrs. Parks said "No," and in so doing she broke the law. She was arrested immediately. The news of her arrest spread quickly.

A meeting was called to organize a protest, and the community chose Martin Luther King Jr. as the leader. He did not want the job, but these historic events as well as the community's "call" made it impossible for him to turn away. Like the Old Testament prophet Isaiah, King declared, "I will not keep silent." As the Old Testament prophet Isaiah proclaimed that Zion would have a new name in recognition of her transformation, King, likewise, proclaimed that America would experience a transformation within its people and within its social infrastructure. Rosa Parks sat down so that King could rise up and share the new name for America that came to him in a dream. He said at the 1963 March on Washington,

> I say to you today, my friends . . . even though we face the dif-
> ficulties of today and tomorrow, I still have a dream. It is a
> dream deeply rooted in the American dream.
>
> I have a dream that one day this nation will rise up and
> live out the true meaning of its creed: We hold these truths to
> be self-evident, that all men [and women] are created
> equal."[3]

Just as Isaiah knew that God would rejoice over the transformation of Zion, King knew that God would rejoice over the transformation of America and the world. When King received the Nobel Peace Prize in 1964 he said:

> Sooner or later, all people of the world will have to discover a
> way to live together in peace. . . . If this is to be achieved, peo-
> ple must evolve for all human conflict a method which rejects
> revenge, aggression and retaliation. The foundation of such a
> message is love. . . . I refuse to accept the cynical notion that

nation after nation must spiral down a militaristic stairway into the hell of thermonuclear destruction. I believe that unarmed truth and unconditional love will have the final work in reality.[4]

King's vivid image of a "militaristic stairway into the hell of thermonuclear destruction" proved precisely perceptive and boldly visionary. In the spring of 1965, President Lyndon Baines Johnson shifted taxpayers' monies further away from domestic social programs, funneling more dollars into the U.S. military-industrial system. Johnson unleashed Operation Rolling Thunder to increase the bombing and killing of the North Vietnamese people. On the same day Johnson intensified that violent offensive, King advanced his pro-love, antiwar stance at Howard University. At the famous black school in the nation's capital, King broke his silence, questioning the wisdom and morality of the U.S. government's public position that advocated a negotiated settlement while simultaneously dropping bombs of death on North Vietnam. King stepped forward on a potentially hazardous path. He attempted to navigate between an increased critique of U.S. federal warmongering and a not-too-isolating discourse that stopped short of alienating the president from the Civil Rights Movement.

Still dodging a wholesale negative jeremiad against the war (which he would finally preach on April 4, 1967), King did highlight the dialectical cause-and-effect interplay between aggressive war and domestic policy, between hatred and love. Restated, he deployed the proverbial "guns versus butter" analogy. The more Johnson yielded to the pressures of special interests signified primarily by the military-industrial lobbyists, the more resources went into war and hate instead of domestic social programs and love. Before proclaiming an unequivocal antiwar posture, King worked successfully with the Southern Christian Leadership Conference's (SCLC) board of directors to craft a group position in opposition to the war. In the fall of 1966, furthermore, King linked international policy with the social plight of America's poor. By the end of that year, the initial seeds took root in what later would become the spring 1968 Poor People's Campaign. He had moved more forcefully in his stand with those victimized by poverty brought about by the wealthy elite. In those memorable remarks, he said:

> Now let us begin. Now let us re-dedicate ourselves to the long and bitter—but beautiful—struggle for a new world. This is the calling of the children of God, and our brother and sisters wait eagerly for our response. Shall we say the odds are too great? Shall we tell them the struggle is too hard? Will our message be that the focus of American life militates against their arrival as full women and men, and we send our deepest regrets? Or will there be another message of longing, of hope, of solidarity with their yearning, of commitment to their cause, whatever the cost? The choice is ours, and though we might prefer it otherwise we *must* choose in this crucial moment of human history.[5]

This April 1967 anti–Vietnam War speech indicated several maturation moments in King's growing anti–U.S. government and anti-wealthy posture. First, he began to use more sharply contrasting, militant metaphors. That is, he linked more tightly his call to the federal government to cease the aggressive unjust war against the Vietnamese people with his call for a righteous war on poverty at home. Second, King reanalyzed previous notions of a prescription for white racism. Earlier in his civil rights career, he called for repeated pricking of the white supremacist's moral conscience. The love dynamic created such a result. Out of Christian love, blacks were repeatedly called on to allow racist whites to continually batter black bodies. By persistently maiming and murdering blacks, the Christian love of God (buried deep below white supremacy's surface) would eventually break through white hatred of black life. The key to transformation is pricking white people's moral conscience.

By the 1967 "Beyond Vietnam" speech, King wondered if the whole nation's moral conscience could be pricked. We find evidence in the tone of his concluding testimony before a Senate committee at year's end. He explained gravely, "The attainment of security and equality for Negroes has not yet become a serious and irrevocable national purpose. I doubt that there was ever a sincere and unshakable commitment to this end."[6]

The Poor People's Campaign: Faith in Action

Eight months after the Vietnam speech, King inaugurated the Poor People's Campaign when he asserted the following: "America is at a crossroads of history, and it is critically important to us, as a nation and a society, to choose a new path and move upon it with resolution and courage. It is impossible to underestimate the crisis we face in America. The stability of civilization, the potential of free government, and the simple honor of [people] are at stake."[7] From then on, he hammered home an Armageddon metaphor. For instance, the words of his April 1968 article for *Look* magazine reveal this observation.

> We intend, before the summer comes, to initiate a "last chance" project to arouse the American conscience toward constructive democratic change. The nation has been warned by the President's Commission (on Civil Disorders) that our society faces catastrophic division in an approaching dooms-day if the country does not act. We have, through this non-violent action, an opportunity to avoid a national disaster and to create a new spirit of harmony.[8]

King advanced his idea to draw together a "multi-racial poor people's movement"[9] whose objective was to rearrange systems of wealth in the United States. He argued, "Timid supplication for justice will not solve the problem. We've got to confront the power structure massively."[10]

In King's mind, the Poor People's Campaign meant terminating the Vietnam War and instead waging an aggressive domestic "war on poverty." He linked the huge war chest spent in Vietnam and the insignificant resources expended on a national anti-poverty program. The initiation of the Poor People's Campaign moved SCLC beyond civil rights for African Americans and toward ideas of economic relief for impoverished Americans.[11] King grounded his reasons for the PPC on moral issues, acknowledging that the campaign would intentionally bring to the surface ideas of class conflict. King knew that any attempt to redistribute wealth would be a long and challenging process. He proceeded in spite of the Goliath standing before him because his moral convictions demanded it. He believed, as did the ancients before him, in the inherent worth and dignity of all persons and the biblical call of God's preferential treatment for the poor.

King's three-pronged plan for the Poor People's Campaign was decisive and hard-hitting. First, a multiracial shantytown would be erected and poor people from across the nation dwelling there would make visible to America issues of poverty. In addition, daily demonstrations were planned along with a major march drawing thousands of people to the nation's capital. Second, mass arrests would demonstrate the seriousness with which ordinary citizens took the issue of redistribution of wealth. Third, a national boycott of various corporations was planned to signal that business would not continue as usual as long as poor people were exploited in a country exploding with wealth.

From Washington D.C. to Memphis

In an event that would barely make the evening news, black sanitation workers in Memphis, Tennessee, called a garbage strike on February 11, 1968. It was underplayed, that is, until Dr. Martin Luther King, prophetic in voice and action, joined the effort. Suddenly, media crews arrived on the scene and displayed dramatically the experiences of the black garbage workers. Gerald McKnight in his book *The Last Crusade* reported:

> The two men, trapped by a torrential rainstorm, took shelter in the barrel of their truck because city police forbade black employees from seeking refuge on the porches of white patrons along the collection route. A freak accident triggered a defective automatic bailer, and they were ground up like garbage. The horror of the tragedy was compounded by the disclosure that their families were not entitled to any benefits because the men were unclassified workers. Local 1733 held a strike meeting on Sunday, February 11. . . . The next day, fewer than 200 sanitation employees reported to work.[12]

On March 18, King addressed an assembly of fifteen thousand at the Masonic Temple in Memphis. He tied the labor strike into his larger focus on economic justice and gave voice to citizens frustrated with unfair labor practices. He challenged grassroots people to stop working and shut the city down. Most significantly, he pledged to spearhead a demonstration that would turn the situation around. King grafted this originally minor local labor dispute into the growing civil rights struggle, specifically the struggle for economic rights.

On March 28, less than two weeks later, King returned to Memphis to lead a protest march to buttress the garbage workers. This march, however, turned violent. Those in the movement claimed that civil authorities, ranging from local police to the FBI, initiated the violence and must be held accountable for it. The powerful press, however, blamed King, and hinted at the possibility of more violence at the upcoming Poor People's Campaign rally in Washington. Instead of deserting the Memphis campaign and drawing back from adverse national media exposure, King began without delay to implement a strategy for another march there. King would not give up on the local people of Memphis; they deserved the commitment of the Poor People's Campaign.

King's passion was deeply tied to the Memphis March, rescheduled for April 8, 1968. On April 4, King was assassinated. As Joseph learned from his brothers, and as the prophets learned too well, violence kills the dreamers.

The Poor People's Campaign Continues

Despite the death of Martin Luther King Jr., the SCLC, under the leadership of Reverend Ralph Abernathy, continued the Poor People's Campaign. Abernathy launched the 1968 march with the proclamation that "The poor are no longer divided. We are not going to let the white man put us down anymore. It's not white power, and I'll give you some news, it's not black power, either. It's poor power and we're going to use it."[13]

Supporters of the Poor People's Campaign collected and delivered to Washington poor people from varied ethnic and national identities and different geographic, cultural, and social locations.

The press tried to be supportive of delegations of the poor descending upon Washington, but ultimately demonstrated great discomfort with the idea and actions of the campaign. The *Washington Post* opined that the "liberal" intentions of the campaign would be more effectively served if "poison spots of poverty" were visited rather than the nation's capital.[14] Officials rarely welcome prophets into the town square. The U.S. government could claim to fight a war against poverty, as long as the victims of the war tactics remained out of sight. The truth proved to be too dangerous for the comfortable in the capital.

The Dream Continues

The radical, Spirit-filled King devoted his life to preaching Good News to the poor and letting the oppressed go free. He had a dream that will not be fulfilled until God's preferential treatment for the poor becomes commonplace, woven into every sinew and synapse of the American people.

We stand, in 2004, as tangled as ever in wars of poverty and international invasion. The poverty level under President George W. Bush increases with each official report. Likewise, the defense budget grows to levels almost unfathomable. Also, we must not forget the increase in body counts from both wars. The dream of the prophets, ancient and modern, of Hebrew and African descent, cries for laborers to proclaim dignity and life in the face of degradation and death.

The dream continues. Who will step forward in faith to finish the race against poverty; to finish the work of the prophet? What will it take for us to heed the call of the prophets before us, to act as if we believe the dream of King—which is, after all, the same dream God gives to prophets of every age. The dream continues. The marches continue. May we care enough to see the poor among and within us, and make the dream materialize, for the sake of the world.

chapter 3

From Prophetic Preaching to Utopian Community

Robert M. Franklin

———

It is the most famous sermon in modern American history. It didn't have a title as such, or a single biblical text, but we know it as the "I Have a Dream" speech. In that brief message, a young African American Baptist preacher from the South stood before America and challenged it to repent. He challenged America to rediscover its own neglected religious heritage and to lay aside the social sins of racism, indifference towards the poor, and obsession with violence. He dreamed *for* America, and in sharing his dream *of* America he invited others to embrace it and work to make it a reality.

An Arresting Portrait

Look again at the familiar portrait of Dr. King delivering his speech from the steps of the Lincoln Memorial. The image is so familiar that we may fail to grasp its extraordinary, multidimensional character. The speaker's podium where King stood was situated just yards away from the feet of Abraham Lincoln, who sits uncomfortably in his great stone chair. Look closer and you might see King restraining the high voltage of his own sectarian religious passion and instead harnessing it in the service of the common good. Some Christians today might feel that he missed an opportunity to preach Christ to the nation. Others feel that that is precisely what he was doing as he pleaded with the nation to include people of color throughout national life, to eradicate the poverty that marred so many lives, and to stop resorting to violence to solve human conflict. And given the example of his own public ministry throughout the South, was this not applied Christianity?

Continue to examine the portrait and you may see a representative of the Christian tradition standing in solidarity with other faith traditions. His theology and his personal witness seemed to proclaim that Christ could live alongside other religions without trying to vanquish or do harm to them. Rather, Christ's inclination would be to respect them and perhaps transform them through love. Francis of Assisi put it well when he said, "Preach the gospel always; use words when necessary."

And one may perceive in the King/Lincoln juxtaposition the mysterious power of religious faith to transform both of these men, and indeed all frail human beings, into courageous exemplars of moral citizenship.

In that 1963 portrait, Lincoln is frozen silent, a figure carved and captured in marble, his complexity and contradictions concealed in cold stone. But in front of the stone stood a vibrant incarnation of the indomitable African American quest for authentic freedom, a symbol of the universal human aspiration for fulfillment.

Listen to some of the opening words of the famous speech. "Five score years ago, a great American, in whose symbolic shadow we stand today, signed the Emancipation Proclamation. This momentous decree came as a beacon light of hope to millions of Negro slaves, who had been seared in the flames of withering injustice. It came as a joyous daybreak to end the long night of their captivity. But one hundred years later, the Negro still is not free." With those words King paid respect to one of the nation's sacred ancestors, underscored the rude fact that Lincoln's agenda was unfinished, and presented himself as a moral ally, if not successor, to the departed president.

How does a preacher address such a diverse audience without alienating or offending those who would not share his theological orientation? For all of its merits and downsides, King's strategy was founded on the Jeffersonian premise that some "truths we all hold to be self-evident." So he drew upon the two major intellectual traditions that have shaped American culture and character: the covenant tradition based upon biblical notions of American exceptionalism; and the Enlightenment tradition of Immanuel Kant, John Locke, Thomas Jefferson, and others who embraced the rational foundations for morality and asserted the inviolable rights of the individual. No one was more skilled at interweaving great ideas from varying sources.

Recall his words that day as he placed his dream in the context of the hard work that lay before his listeners. "Even though we must face the difficulties of today and tomorrow, I still have a dream. It is a dream deeply rooted in the American dream . . . that one day this nation will rise up and live out the true meaning of its creed: We hold these truths to be self-evident, that all men are created equal." King believed that a dream inspired by particularist, biblical sources could live in dialectical and fruitful tension with ideals embraced by nontheistic rationalists. "I have a dream that one day every valley shall be exalted, and every hill and mountain shall be made low, the rough places will be made plain, and the crooked places will be made straight and the glory of the Lord shall be revealed and all flesh shall see it together."

King understood that the key to building a multicultural and multiracial beloved community required some common texts, common experience, common moral sense—in short, common ground—which he and others would have to evoke, if it happened to exist but in a latent state. Or he might have to imagine and propose common ground out of the ideas available to him. He read widely. He listened to, and learned from, thought leaders from other religious traditions. And he had a voracious and catholic intellect always reaching out, always available for transformation by truth lodged in traditions different from his own. Yet his unifying vision led him to see that truth is monistic. It emanates from a single, common source. The human task is to gather up our fragments of truth that lie dispersed in various places and, through dialogue, seek to apprehend its underlying unity. King was a Christian who learned from a Hindu, Mohandas K. Gandhi. He was a Southerner who readily embraced allies in the North. He was a black man who found common ground with white, Asian, Indian, Arab, Latino, and other members of the human family.

By doing so, King was able to use theology and ethics as resources for renewing American public life. His public theology prompted people to vote, to run for office, and to be concerned about the moral hygiene of the society. A person who seeks to create common ground, build traditions, craft narratives, and negotiate coalitions exemplifies a quality of character that moral education should seek to inculcate.

We should also acknowledge that using theology and ethics as resources for renewing public life can have unforeseen negative consequences. For instance, many religious people who regard the concept of grace as central to their faith may construe it to mean that they are acceptable to God despite their admitted and continuing racist behavior and attitudes or their indifference to the moral value of racial justice. Such status quo apologists often argue that America has come a long way since the 1960s, expending huge amounts of goodwill and national resources. Thus, those who feel restless about advancing further should now lay off to allow the nation to consolidate these gains, rather than experience further instability. We should now let sleeping dogs lie and celebrate our collective progress. They admit that there are still disparities and isolated instances of virulent racism. But on the whole, the nation is better; hence impatient activists and militants should simply "get over it" and accept the new reality. God has forgiven America for its evil past, and we are now back on target to become the city on a hill for the nations to emulate.

This is where doctrines of the Christian tradition can be distorted for specific political and ideological purposes. Grace becomes a psychological mechanism to absolve responsibility for the present condition of racial and economic disparity of opportunity. This is the double edge of grace. Ironically, the theological shift from "salvation by conscientious works" (evident during the Civil Rights Movement) to "salvation by grace" authorizes complacency with the racial status quo. Theologically speaking, this is not a basis for replacing grace with human effort. Rather, it serves as a reminder that sacred scripture and theological concepts can be misappropriated to justify social evil. We must all beware of this seductive tendency in our lives and in the communities where we live and worship. King, like other liberal evangelical theologians, believed that the Bible and human reason should and must live in creative tension sustained by ongoing, mutually critical dialogue.

Now I'd like to do two things: First, sketch briefly the congregational culture that nurtured Martin Luther King and so many other citizens whose names we do not know but to whom we are all indebted for a rehabilitated democracy. My point will be that all congregations can and should nurture individuals to develop into responsible moral agents. The question will be, is this happening in the congregation that you call home? Critical to this process is the quality of church leadership, both clergy and lay. I trust that many in the seminaries are committed to preparing such leaders. This point will also serve to illustrate how a poor, marginalized, and almost invisible religious community, namely the black church, helped to renew all of American democracy, not simply advance the interests of black people. Second, I will look more carefully at Dr. King's idea of the "beloved community," his language for multicultural America, as an ethical norm. Ethical norms can be used to evaluate, to critique, to guide, and to transform individual behavior as well as public policy. I will conclude with some brief comments about the heroic role that faith communities can and must play at this critical moment in history.

The Revolution Led by Preachers, Churchwomen, and Sunday School Children

Paul Tillich said that culture is the form of religion, and religion is the substance of culture. To understand Dr. King's journey from Atlanta to the steps of the Lincoln Memorial in 1963, we need to understand something about the culture that produced him, and thereby revisit the ways in which culture is a vehicle of moral education.

King's biographers all note that the black church and family were the contexts in which the boy King learned something about racism, poverty, and religion as a resource for mobilizing social change. James H. Cone has gone further to note that the culture of the black church included serious theological concepts that played a critical role in shaping King's worldview and moral compass. These included notions of human freedom, social justice, black self-love, and collective power.

Historians such as Albert Raboteau (Princeton), the late James Melvin Washington (Union), and Evelyn Brooks Higginbotham (Harvard) have noted that black church culture is an amalgam of many symbolic and ritual traditions, particularly of four distinct traditions: African traditional religions, Catholic popular piety, Protestant evangelicalism, and Islam. This collection of symbolic traditions infused the core practices of progressive African American Christianity, which produced King.

The ecology of black folk congregations usually includes the core religious practices. First is a multi-sensory worship experience in which nearly all of the human senses are stimulated for response. If the senses are perceived as receptors of divine communication, it is rational to design and sponsor worship that communicates at a variety of levels, not merely the cognitive and visual. In most black churches, worship is a *sacred drama*; it may even include a dance with the gods. Hence *drums* are typically played to orchestrate the antiphonal call and response between the people and God. Drums have a special significance for people of African descent in America because they were prohibited by law, especially once slave masters learned that Africans could communicate across distant spaces, not only with God but also with one another. By contrast, slavery in Brazil did not forbid drumming, and today one witnesses in Afro-Brazilian worship—and certainly in the annual carnival—amazing polyrhythms and sensuous celebration.

But wait: not only are the ears and bodies of worshippers encouraged to rejoice, there is always a *visual feast*. Colorful choir robes and clergy vestments replace the often bleak, cold, and gray urban environments in which many church members live and work. Entering church on Sunday is akin to entering the colorful kingdom described in the Apocalypse of the New Testament. Some, not all, black churches go further. Brass horns, electric guitars, tambourines, liturgical dancers, clapping hands, and praise teams electrify the air with sound. And why ignore the olfactory sense? Here I refer not to the pungency of liturgical incense but to the productions of the church kitchen next door. There, faithful and talented church mothers and deacons are worshipping amidst an orchestra of steaming pots and pans, sending the alluring aromas of fried chicken, collard greens, corn bread, candied yams, and peach cobbler wafting throughout the neighborhood. Even black worshippers in northern climes such as Chicago, Minneapolis, and New York can feel magically transported to the southern lands where their ancestors toiled and learned to cook this way. What's more, white worshippers who visit black churches on the right Sunday can partake of this expanded interpretation of the eucharistic table. Furthermore, this sacred space is animated by lots of touching, hugging, holy kissing, and high-five greetings that eliminate—some would say invade—the usual social distance and personal space that most of us regard as sacred.

Embedded within this thick and rich liturgical ethos is a second practice whose transforming effect is easily overlooked, namely, the art of intimate communal prayer. *Intimate* and *communal* almost constitute an oxymoron. Those signifiers point to opposite zones of the human sociality. *Intimate* denotes the small, secretive, and personal space you share with your very best confidants, family, and friends. Is this why Plato suggested you could not have more than a couple of best friends? There's not enough time, or space. (Unless you happen to be Bill Clinton, who annually invited about two hundred of his very best friends to the White House, and each year it was a different two hundred.)

Communal suggests a zone of inclusive capacity. We can all fit in here; we can all share this. Communal prayer invites people to move and to touch. Typically, worshippers are urged to leave their seats (secure and familiar space) to gather at the altar with strangers, lots of them. Then you may kneel or be asked to hold the hand of the stranger nearby. The drama builds as individuals bow to address God. Then the worship leader begins, "*Our* Father who art in heaven . . . we are your children once again, standing in the need of prayer." As the prayer leader articulates the travails and tragedies of the human condition (usually in a noble sixteenth-century King

James idiom), the individual worshipper fills in the blanks noting her or his own personal agenda, needs, and gratitude. Something grace-filled happens in that milieu. Holding the hand of another person while reckoning with my own personal stuff may remind me that I'm not alone; others are struggling too. And maybe while I'm at it, I'll pray for him or her too. Phenomenologically, it is impossible to determine precisely when or where or how it happens. But people testify to the fact that such prayer succeeds in weaving detached, autonomous individuals into a community of shared pain, hope, and solidarity. Worshippers who cautiously approached the altar alone in their thoughts return to their seats as connected and re-membered in the body of Christ.

A third core element of black church culture can be characterized as triumphal praise and occurs as choirs lead the congregation's confident chant that it will not be vanquished by evil in the world. Triumphal songs express the eschatological hope that their temporal struggles and their faithful service as soldiers in the "army of the Lord" actually mean something. Their lives matter. Even if they're little girls attending Sunday school in a Birmingham church when a bomb explodes a quiet Sunday morning. Unnamed martyrs count in salvation history.

I think of myself as a progressive Christian ethicist and theologian. That means that I'm willing to explore just how far the radical love ethic of Jesus takes us in transforming God's creation, if we trust the Holy Spirit to sort out the details. As such, I am cautious about triumphal Christian language. As we all know, Christian triumphalism has a speckled past. It fortified many of the saints who spread the gospel to faraway, strange lands. But in its course it often left a trail of blood and a very bad reputation for Jesus of Nazareth. How could this God of love authorize the events of the Crusades? Or recall the smaller tragedy of such triumphalism brilliantly described by Barbara Kingsolver in her moving novel *The Poisonwood Bible*. So I understand why some might flinch at the use of this term *triumphal*. Yet if you view this usage from the perspective of those who have been enslaved and recently freed but haunted by long memories, then celebrating the journey from oppression to liberation seems fitting.

The final feature of black church culture is also distinctive: prophetic preaching. Many of you know that the black sermon is an art form shared, delivered, performed only by skilled virtuosi. Often copied but never replicated, it is the high, holy moment in the liturgical drama. The brilliant historian of religion Mircea Eliade observed that "for people in traditional societies religion is a means of extending the world spatially upward so that communication with the other world becomes ritually possible, and extending it temporally backward so that the paradigmatic acts of the gods and mythical ancestors can be continually re-enacted and indefinitely recoverable."[1] Eliade helps to illumine the genius of black preaching as he reminds us that words can be deployed to mediate an encounter with the holy. Words can open the imagination into a transcendent realm, where one may be empowered to give one's life on behalf of a noble cause. The black preacher—through the virtuosity of imaginative, narrative, lyrical, and poetic language and through the co-creativity of a responsive congregation—unites the sacred and the human realms.

Again, the point of this description and analysis of this particular congregational culture is to highlight the manner in which the liturgical culture of progressive black churches nurtured virtues necessary in citizens to sustain democracy. Such congregations, whatever their ethnic or cultural identity, help to form moral character and citizenship habits that translate into a willingness to make personal sacrifices that might benefit future generations. It is a virtue that the psychologist Erik Erikson referred to as "generativity." On this basis, I would make the normative claim that good and faithful congregations nurture generativity, especially among their adult members.

Biblical scholar Walter Brueggemann offers a cogent observation about such transformative liturgy: "Every act of a minister who would be prophetic is part of a way of evoking, forming, and reforming an alternative community. And this applies to every facet and every practice of ministry. It is a measure of our enculturation that the various acts of ministry (for example, counseling, administration, even liturgy) have taken on lives and functions of their own rather than being seen as elements of the one prophetic ministry of formation and reformation of alternative community."[2]

Brueggemann's comment about "alternative community" reminds us again of King's dream narrative, and the fact that it was crafted in the genre of a sermon rather than as essay, philosophical argument, or lecture. King and his counterparts were products of a liturgical culture that cultivated the capacity to engage in utopian discourse and to act boldly to achieve moral causes.

We will explore more about utopian discourse, black Christian preaching, and political theology when we turn to King's notion of the beloved community.

The Underside of American Christianity

It is perplexing to consider that Christianity has had two thousand years to eradicate the multiple and overlapping forms of oppression based upon ethnicity, race, creed, culture, region, class, and gender but has failed to do so. Why is this the case? And more to the point of our discussion, why haven't Protestantism and Catholicism succeeded in canceling the power and grip of racism on the minds and behavior of their own members? Is this a theological crisis? Does the tradition possess the resources to address racism in a compelling manner? Is it a human and cultural crisis that represents, yet again, the depths and variety of human sinful nature? King framed it poignantly when he noted in his "Letter from a Birmingham Jail,"

> I have traveled the length and breadth of Alabama, Mississippi and all the other southern states. On sweltering summer days and crisp autumn mornings I have looked at the South's beautiful churches with their lofty spires pointing heavenward. I have beheld the impressive outlines of her massive religious-education buildings. Over and over I have found myself asking: "What kind of people worship here? Who is their God? Where were their voices when the lips of Governor Barnett dripped with words of interposition and nullification? Where were they when Governor Wallace gave a clarion call for defiance and hatred? Where were their voices of support when bruised and weary Negro men and

women decided to rise from the dark dungeons of complacency to the bright hills of creative protest?"[3]

Although prophetic religion should hold the state accountable
for the moral exercise of power, when religion goes astray, who
calls it back to its foundations? This is where King's methodologi-
cal and symbolic eclecticism proved valuable. The biblical and
Enlightenment traditions should critique and correct each other.
New knowledge from the natural and social sciences, contemporary cultural information, and local communities should be put
into dialogue with the revelation of sacred scripture. Dialogue
aided by prayer and reflection and other disciplines of the spirit
can help us to get it right. Here some may object to this method,
often referred to by theologians as the "revised correlational
method" as elaborated by the University of Chicago Catholic theologian David Tracy. Scripture is not meant to be spoken back to,
they declare, but obeyed. And yet, absent such dialogue, fallible
human beings may interpret scripture's gifts in ways that do harm
and fundamentally contradict the love that God offers the world
through Christ. It took a fallible Christian as courageous as St. Paul
to admit that he had been wrong about his previous views of the
Jesus movement. It took a lot for Peter to admit tearfully that he
had misinterpreted a holy revelation when he excluded Gentiles
from Christian fellowship. This invites us to consider: have we, too,
been guilty of some errant interpretation or application of Christ's
teaching that has diminished rather than enhanced Christ's lordship in the world?

Returning to my earlier reference to King's preaching as an
instance of utopian discourse, I would like to discuss briefly the
central norm in King's political theology.

The Beloved Community as a Political and Ethical Norm

Moral philosopher and former Clinton domestic policy advisor
William Galston has noted that "utopian thought is the political
branch of moral philosophy." Among its many functions, he
claims, are "to guide our deliberation in devising courses of action,

justify our actions so that the grounds of action are reasons that others ought to accept, and serve as the basis for the evaluation of existing institutions and practices."[4] Utopian discourse becomes moral discourse as it seeks to guide action. It enables us to "imaginatively reconcile and transmute" the "contradictions of experience."

In his final book, *Where Do We Go From Here: Chaos or Community?*, King elaborated his vision of a better nation and world. He wrote, the "good and just society is neither the thesis of capitalism nor the antithesis of Communism, but a *socially conscious democracy* which reconciles the truths of individualism and collectivism." He characterized his political philosophy with the term *democratic socialism*, a concept that solicited the suspicion and harassment of J. Edgar Hoover's FBI. In his November 1966 Gandhi Memorial Lecture at Howard University, he said, "Public accommodations did not cost the nation anything; the right to vote did not cost the nation anything. Now we are grappling with basic class issues between the privileged and underprivileged. In order to solve this problem, not only will it mean the restructuring of American society but it will cost the nation something."[5]

King had always been attentive to the economic dimensions of authentic liberation. At the end of his life, his public ministry focused upon highlighting the nation's moral obligations to improve the economic plight of the least advantaged members of the community, to borrow a phrase from the eminent and recently deceased Harvard philosopher John Rawls. When he was killed in Memphis, King was working on behalf of sanitation workers, and he was headed back to Washington D.C. to lead a national "Poor People's Campaign." Ironically, had he lived, there would have been another great speech and, perhaps, another iconic photograph to juxtapose with the 1963 image.

King's public ministry began with a situational focus upon desegregating public transportation and achieving racial justice in the South. Over time, his emphasis broadened to focus on economic justice and global peace. He did not choose this form of public ministry. It stalked and chose him. Perhaps this should be a sobering reminder to all who find themselves in relatively comfortable zones of ministry and vocation. The spirit of the times can find us, unsettle us, and demand that we drop what we are doing to take up God's cause. Friends and family are likely to judge such shifts as erratic and irresponsible. But those who have made and changed history understand that their actions are responsible because they are being responsive to the One who has made deep claims upon their existence.

It is humbling, hopeful, and empowering to consider that preachers, churchwomen, and Sunday school children led a revolution in our lifetime. They marched, prayed, voted, and challenged the nation to, in the words of Arthur Schlesinger Jr., "conform America's political reality to her political rhetoric." They have now passed the baton to us.

As we face the uncertainties and fears of our time, remember the words of C. S. Lewis: "Courage is not one of the virtues, it is the form of all the virtues at their testing point."

chapter 4

Growing like Topsy
Solidarity in a Multicultural U.S.A.

Emilie M. Townes

———

She was one of the blackest of her race; and her round shin-
ing eyes, glittering as glass beads, moved with quick and restless glances over everything in the room. Her mouth, half
open with astonishment at the wonders of the new Mas'r's
parlor, displayed a white and brilliant set of teeth. Her woolly
hair was braided in sundry little tails, which stuck out in
every direction. The expression of her face was an odd mixture of shrewdness and cunning, over which was oddly
drawn, like a kind of veil, an expression of the most doleful
gravity and solemnity. She was dressed in a single filthy,
ragged garment, made of bagging; and stood with her hands
demurely folded before her. Altogether, there was something
odd and goblin-like about her appearance—something, as
Miss Ophelia afterwards said, "so heathenish," as to inspire
that good lady with utter dismay; and turning to St. Clare,
she said, "Augustine, what in the world have you brought that
thing here for?"[1]
—Harriet Beecher Stowe, *Uncle Tom's Cabin*

These are truly interesting times to be thinking about our multicultural
America. Rather than see it as our future, I think it has become clear,
with the most recent Census Bureau statistics released in 2003, that
we are already multicultural. Media reports have announced that

Hispanics (which include Mexicans, Puerto Ricans, Cubans, Central and South Americans, and those of other Latino/a origins—who can be of any race or one of several nationalities) have now passed blacks as the largest minority group. Although that gap is now small—37 million to 36.2 million—the projections are that this will increase over the next ten years.

But the actual statistics reveal a more nuanced reality. For the first time in 2000, census respondents could choose more than one race in identifying themselves. This fact alone should let us know that we *are* multicultural as a society. In addition, the number of Americans declaring themselves black either wholly or "in combination with one or more other races" is now 37.7 million—slightly higher than the overall figure for Latino/as.

In short, we are a complex nation, more diverse than we give ourselves credit for. The simple black/white axis we have divided ourselves on with regard to race is an anachronism at best and wholly inadequate at worst.

Given this reality, one of the key issues I think about when considering the great diversity of who we already are, as people of faith, in relation to the vision of Martin Luther King Jr. is the issue of solidarity. Given the challenges of a brutalized economy, a so-called self-legitimating war—one that fails to learn from Israel's six-day self-legitimating war some thirty-five years ago, which is still trapped in its seventh day—and all the rest of what we face these days, thinking and talking about solidarity amidst our differences in the face of such structural evils may seem an exercise in tempting the agony of the absurd.

Stowe's introduction of the character Topsy in her abolitionist novel *Uncle Tom's Cabin* is a case in point. In this vividly troubling introduction of Topsy, Stowe exposes us to the traditional stereotypes of black women slaves (regardless of age). Topsy is black, her eyes are round, and they shine—they actually glitter. Her eyes, not her body, move quickly and restlessly over the contents and the people in the room. Her blackness is contrasted with the brilliant whiteness of her teeth. Her hair is woolly and braided in such a way that her plaits stick out in every direction. Her face is a mixture of shrewdness and cunning, gravity and solemnity. She has a single ragged dress made of bagging. She appears odd and goblin-like, heathenish.

This description of Topsy, noting her "black, glassy eyes [that] glittered with a kind of wicked drollery," puts in print a character who is lazy, mischievous, wild-looking, and prone to thievery. She needs constant guidance and beatings to keep her working and out of trouble. However, Stowe's point is that Topsy is all these things because of the dehumanizing system of slavery, not because of her blackness. Yet Stowe's description of Topsy remains troubling. It is a swill pot of caricature—Topsy is a slave girl who perfectly fits the black stereotype of the time. Stowe's description of Topsy contains imagery of a barely human young girl. Despite all that Stowe attempts to do in speaking out against the institution of slavery, she still clings to imagery that never allows Topsy to be seen as fully human or humane. The reader never comes to know Topsy (or any black female in the novel) as a person, for her character is never developed. Stowe, regrettably, repeats the very dehumanizing process she seeks to critique.

The womanist question is: What happens when Topsy speaks? What happens when Topsy moves from a literary character functioning as a metaphor to a living exemplar of the material history and lives of African American children, men, and women? What does it mean when the crude caricature of the pickaninny who has been described and categorized by others starts to carve out and speak out of an identity in which she is an active agent? What does it mean when the dismantling of evil calls for a commitment to *conscious* reflection on the interplay between culture, identity, community, theory, practice, myth, memory, history, life, death?

It is here where my work as a Christian ethicist seeks to understand the absurd metaphors encircling our lives in an America that often feels far distant from King's dream or mountaintop. For me, womanist ethics helps us remember and explore the fact that inclusion does not guarantee justice, and access to an inequitable and grossly maldistributed social order does not mean the transformation of fragmented communities, or of whole ones.

This is not a dream, but a nightmare.

So how might we lean into, walk into, run into, crawl into, and shimmy into a truly liberatory space—a space in which Topsy and all her kin and friends can speak? A place that invites listening and hearing? A space that that takes seriously turning dreams into realities? A space that invites us to dare faithfulness, to drop our defenses, to accept responsibility to live in genuine accountability? Because we know that if *we* do not right the wrongs of the past (or at least attempt to), we leave it to future generations—and this is a gruesome legacy to pass on as a gift.

The Village We Are

In her 1990 "State of the Village Report" article, the late environmentalist Donella Meadows describes our world if we shrank the earth's population to one thousand people with all the existing human ratios remaining the same. Some of her findings:

> 584 would be Asians
> 123 would be Africans
> 95 would be East and West Europeans
> 84 Latin Americans
> 55 Soviets (still including for the moment Lithuanians, Latvians, Estonians, etc.)
> 52 North Americans
> 6 Australians and New Zealanders . . .
> 300 Christians (183 Catholics, 84 Protestants, 33 Orthodox)
> 175 Moslems
> 128 Hindus
> 55 Buddhists
> 47 Animists
> 210 all other religions (including atheists) . . .
> One-third (330) of the people in the village would be children. Half the children would be immunized against the preventable infectious diseases such as measles and polio. Sixty of the thousand villagers would be over the age of 65. Just under half of the married women would have access to and be using modern contraceptives. Each year 28 babies would be born.

Each year 10 people would die, three of them for lack of food, one from cancer. Two of the deaths would be to babies born within the year. One person in the village would be infected with the HIV virus; that person would most likely not yet have developed a full-blown case of AIDS. With the 28 births and 10 deaths, the population of the village in the next year would be 1018.

In this thousand-person community, 200 people would receive three-fourths of the income; another 200 would receive only 2% of the income. Only 70 people would own an automobile (some of them more than one automobile). About one-third would not have access to clean, safe drinking water. Of the 670 adults in the village half would be illiterate. . . .

If the world were a village of 1000 persons, there would be five soldiers, seven teachers, one doctor. Of the village's total annual expenditures of just over $3 million per year, $181,000 would go for weapons and warfare, $159,000 for education, $132,000 for health care.

The village would have buried beneath it enough explosive power in nuclear weapons to blow itself to smithereens many times over. These weapons would be under the control of just 100 of the people. The other 900 people would be watching them with deep anxiety, wondering whether the 100 can learn to get along together, and if they do, whether they might set off the weapons anyway through inattention or technical bungling, and if they ever decide to dismantle the weapons, where in the village they will dispose of the dangerous radioactive materials of which the weapons are made.[2]

These kind of global markers are helpful because we often get caught in our domestic or national or state or local lives with myopic hearts and miserly minds that keep us from seeing the richness of who we are as people of faith, as members of a large country that is a world power. We are tempted to stop far too short of exploring who we really are and how we prepare for ministry and how we do ministry in light of this.

This has always been an unwise tactic, but it turns deadly in the kind of climate we have today, which tempts us to gaze closer and closer at our navels rather than insist that we, as people of faith, ask tough questions about where we are headed as nations, as religious bodies, as local and global citizens, as seekers of the spirit, as doers of the word. We are tempted to do a religious version of turning down the main power generator to conserve energy, and we can engage in some of the most internecine and inane turf battles while forgetting the flood, the locusts, the five hundred prophets of Baal, the Hebrew prophets, the disciples, the rainbow. For better or worse, we have the not-so-enviable task of reminding folks what we are called to do as people of faith, as leaders in a wide variety of ministry settings to religious bodies that are, far too often, either captive to or taking captives in a status quo that does not call out the best in us.

But this is only one side of the picture.

I am also amazed at the incredible ways in which many churches roll up their sleeves, see the resources that they have as gifts (not limitations), and proceed to do faith-filled ministry that makes a difference not only in the lives it touches but in the lives of those who are doing the touching. These are ministries that are alive with the spirit; that find ways to keep the door open to God's ongoing revelation. These churches, large and small and in between, combine spirituality and justice as imperatives for faithful living. They do the mundane things: they not only allow homeless folk to sleep on their steps, they invite them in to keep warm and perhaps even fed—and not only at the prescribed times, if the church offers a meals or shelter program. They take large endowments and use more than the prescribed 4.5 percent drawdown rate on the interest earned to expand their social ministries. Not simply by adding new staff, but by getting members of the church involved in the communities in which they worship and perhaps even beyond them—or, even more, by working together with those communities to determine how each church can live out its witness in that place. They take in all manner of folk we send to them from our seminaries and they help us grow them into leaders or help them discover that their call may be something else. These churches challenge us and love us and encourage us while expecting the best from us.

We Didn't Just Grow'd

To return again to Stowe's *Uncle Tom's Cabin*:

> When arrayed at last in a suit of decent and whole clothing, her hair cropped short to her head, Miss Ophelia, with some satisfaction, said she looked more Christian-like than she did, and in her own mind began to mature some plans for her instruction.
>
> Sitting down before her, she began to question her.
>
> "How old are you, Topsy?"
>
> "Dun no, Missis," said the image, with a grin that showed all her teeth.
>
> "Don't know how old you are? Didn't anybody ever tell you? Who was your mother?"
>
> "Never had none!" said the child, with another grin.
>
> "Never had any mother? What do you mean? Where were you born?"
>
> "Never was born!" persisted Topsy, with another grin, that looked so goblin-like, that, if Miss Ophelia had been at all nervous, she might have fancied that she had got hold of some sooty gnome from the land of Diablerie; but Miss Ophelia was not nervous, but plain and business-like, and she said, with some sternness,
>
> "You mustn't answer me in that way, child; I'm not playing with you. Tell me where you were born, and who your father and mother were."
>
> "Never was born," reiterated the creature, more emphatically; "never had no father nor mother, nor nothin'. I was raised by a speculator, with lots of others. Old Aunt Sue used to take care on us. . . ."
>
> "How long have you lived with your master and mistress?"
>
> "Dun no, Missis."
>
> "Is it a year, or more, or less?"
>
> "Dun no, Missis. . . ."
>
> "Have you ever heard anything about God, Topsy?"
>
> The child looked bewildered, but grinned as usual.
>
> "Do you know who made you?"
>
> "Nobody, as I knows on," said the child, with a short laugh.

The idea appeared to amuse her considerably; for her eyes twinkled, and she added,

"I spect I grow'd. Don't think nobody never made me."

"Do you know how to sew?" said Miss Ophelia, who thought she would turn her inquiries to something more tangible.

"No, Missis."[3]

This conversation between the Yankee, Miss Ophelia, and the young black girl slave, Topsy, is instructive and subversive. Throughout the novel, Stowe's gross stereotyping of Topsy also contains a liberatory note. The reader is shown the ways in which Topsy is more than capable of doing her work and learning her lessons. She is revealed as smart and capable—but she is unwilling to do the tasks assigned to her because that is what is expected of her. Topsy chooses to wear the mask the white owners (and Stowe) have given to her.

Is the mask present in the conversation above? It is difficult to know and it is possible to build a case for yes or no. Perhaps this is not the most pressing point, however. In this conversation, Topsy, wittingly or not, subverts Miss Ophelia's ideological assumptions and outright ignorance of the fate of most slaves. It was not unusual for slaves to be unaware of their actual birth date, their parents, or their place of birth. It was also not a matter of rote that a slave would receive Christian religious instruction. Topsy's response speaks to the power of hegemony when it operates with such pervasiveness that it erases memories, and/or it never allows the subjects to know or learn their history. This is a more profound process than historical or social amnesia because the person or the community cannot remember what they never knew.[4]

Cast in a more contemporary light, this attempt by Miss Ophelia to forge a bond with Topsy reminds me, all too often, of those instances when those of us who have some measure of power—either by position in our sociopolitical hierarchy or by dint of our own will—decide to attempt solidarity with groups or individuals who are among the dispossessed because we recognize and embrace the multiculturalism that is already who we are. It is usually a dismal business that ensues. The expected answers are never given, the hoped-for common vision does not emerge, a recalcitrant commitment to justice remains deferred because the genuine differences among us are either glossed over, ignored, treated as impassable barriers, or viewed with an impregnable ignorance that veers into solipsistic ruminations: Why can't they be like us, act like us, talk like us, feel like us, *be us?*

Growing Topsy, living into our future in a country that is growing more and more multicultural every day, means that naive and ill-designed attempts at solidarity are questioned and debunked. As Topsy and her kinfolk and friends pull up their *own* chairs to the postmodern welcome table, and begin to speculate on what it takes to grow, notions of solidarity and multiculturalism and difference must be met face to face. For me, it is crucial that I remember that I cannot speak for all African American women—let alone all black folk. So I want to close with some of my own reflections on what growing like Topsy, or more importantly, growing Topsy means for me when facing the challenges of forging a solidarity in which we stand with one another as pilgrims on a magnificent journey.

I begin with a quote:

> We do not sweat and summon our best in order to rescue the killers; it is to comfort and to empower the possible victims of evil that we do tinker and daydream and revise and memorize, and then impart all that we can of our inspired, our inherited humanity.[5]

These words are from the late black feminist theorist and writer June Jordan. I mull them over, of late, in relation to what they may have to say in reminding me why I do what I do and how and in what ways. For me, to talk about standing with one another, to conjure solidarity across differences in a multicultural world, to spark womanist wisdom on solidarity and differences is, at first glance (and I must admit on several glances, looks, mullings later), to tempt the agony of the absurd. I feel as though I have been cast back in time to that 1960s cocktail party in which Ralph Ellison, the author of *Invisible Man,* spoke in "clipped, deliberate syllables" to his peers.

> "Show me the poem, tell me the names of the opera/the symphony that will stop one man from killing another man and then maybe"—he gestured toward the elegant bejeweled assembly with his hand that held a cut-crystal glass of scotch—"just maybe some of this can be justified."[6]

I am relieved to say that tempting the agony of the absurd does not leave me in Ellison's condemnatory despair but in a frustrated hope. This hope is imbued with Jordan's words as they echo, "We do not sweat and summon our best in order to rescue the killers; it is to comfort and empower the possible victims of evil." There are days, in fact, when I'll be damned if I rescue any killer or someone even approaching such a grotesque status.

To work in solidarity with those who are like me, unlike me, or resemble me does not demand or require that I save those who would see others dead or annihilated either through neglect, indifference, calculation, or theological and ethical musings. I will not rescue the killers of dreams and visions of a world better than this, of hopes that continue to pulse, however faintly, in the midst of disaster and ruin. I will not rescue the killers who create optional reading lists that signal to me that some actual or alleged scholars really believe that there are optional peoples, cultures, lives, ideas, hopes, realities. Secondary lists are little better when they traffic peoples' yearnings and expectations as ideologies and abstractions.

I will not rescue the killers who remain silent when the innocent are murdered and it is called patriotism or ethnic cleansing or white male rage or horizontal violence. Who remain silent when people starve on our streets while there is more than enough food for everyone to eat three squares a day and at least one snack. Who remain silent when children die unloved, unwanted, and thrown away as we shake our collective pious heads and shut the doors of our homes and our hearts. Who remain silent when money determines right and wrong, good and evil, unity and dissent, diversity and blandness, hope and despair, promise and lies, war and peace, damnation and salvation.

No, absolutely no, I will not rescue the killers when the church functions like an efficient corporation, and numbers and spaces in parking lots and the joy of multiple worship services serve as the markers for spirit and love and mercy and justice. Hear me now: I will *not* rescue the killers when the academy—our seminaries—devolves into a gigantic public hog pen for creativity and intellect.

In other words, for me and my house, growing up Topsy while standing with others in multicultural America does not require that I be run over in a mad goal-driven pursuit of a misbegotten notion of solidarity. It does not mean that I accept a specious rule-driven notion of a disinterested love that asks me to sacrifice my very soul so that others may find comfort and ease in the macabre spectacle of my self-abnegation or the obliteration of whole peoples. It is simply unacceptable that any of us acquiesce to a least-common-denominator justice that is really no justice at all.

Justice is not found in answering the question: Can't we all get along? It is found in the elegant but tough notion of King's beloved community. This community is not a lofty utopian goal to be confused with the rapturous image of the peaceable kingdom where lions and lambs coexist in idyllic harmony. The beloved community is a realistic, achievable goal that comes when enough of us join together with not only the vision, but also the commitment and the will that all people can share in the wealth of the earth. This is a community where poverty, hunger, and homelessness will not be tolerated because national and international standards of human decency will not allow it, and where an all-inclusive spirit of sisterhood and brotherhood will replace racism and all forms of discrimination, bigotry, and prejudice. In this community the notion of just war is a vile oxymoron, and love and trust will triumph over fear and hatred. Here, conflicts are seen as an inevitable part of human experience but they are resolved peacefully through hard work, commitment, and mutual respect. Membership in King's beloved community does not require that you or I check our passions, insights, and communities at the door to enter the halls of kumbaya.

And if any wisdom can come from this black woman on notions of solidarity and multiculturalism, it is that to engage in such work is absolutely dangerous. It may, in fact, not be good for one's health at all. It can lead to heart and soul-ache. It can make us old before our time. It can make us eat and drink too much or too little of all the unhealthy things. It can turn us bitter and sarcastic. It can make us ornery and mean as snakes. It can turn justice into vengeance. It can turn *us* into killers.

However, the danger does not stop here. It is dangerous because it *can* mean that *we* refuse the emotional numbing panaceas of acquisition and status and competitive spirit that do not seek excellence, only winning. *We* see through the straw figure of a free market and speak with increasing precision and accuracy about the impact of transnationals—from agribusiness to munitions to clothing manufacturers—and of Western tastes and cultures passing themselves off as neutral or the markers of progress.

We become dangerous when we speak the truth that the king *is* naked when it comes to the U.S. prison industrial complex or when we question declarations of war that are soon accompanied by massive bailouts for corporations that even that bastion of progressive monetary policies, the *Wall Street Journal,* said "mainly padded corporate bottom lines."[7] We become dangerous to a meandering mendacious status quo when we point out that any victory in Iraq won't end the world's distrust of the United States because the second Bush administration has repeatedly abrogated international agreements. In just two years, the Bush administration told Europe it had no interest in dealing with global warming, told Russia to that it had no interest in maintaining our mutual agreements on missile defense, told developing countries that it was not interested in dealing with onerous trade policies regarding lifesaving pharmaceuticals, told Mexico it would not honor the immigration agreements it has forged with it, mortally insulted the Turks, and pulled out of the International Criminal Court.

We become dangerous when we cry foul over the double tax every working American pays in social security and Medicare, a tax that affects 100 million wage earners yet goes unaddressed and unacknowledged in favor of a studied focus on dividends that significantly affect only a small percentage of U.S. households. We are right to question the motives of those folk who conveniently choose literal interpretations of scripture that support their views on homosexuality, abortion, the roles of women and men, the place of clergy and laity, the pillaging of the environment, and just about anything else—except individual and corporate sinning in the name of individualism and the alleged common good. Yes, this is a incandescently naked king when it comes to public policy: policy that is really the personal agenda of moralizing rhetoricians who are dangerous because they now hold elected office. Someone believed that they should bring us back to the good old days, which were, for many of us, deadly.

No, I am not here for the killers when it comes to solidarity—which I assume is another way to say justice. I am not interested in them except to learn how to decrease their numbers and their power. I have no wish to be objective about their behavior, methods, ideologies, or strategies. When I do the work of justice, it is with and as an advocate for the victims—actual, possible, imagined—of evil. This means it is subjective, it is emotional, it is passionate, and it is *very* interested work. If I cannot find others who are interested and committed to this, then there is no solidarity. Our differences do not only separate us—they make us adversaries or enemies.

In other words, I do not *assume* solidarity when I join others in the work of justice in the midst of our present and growing multiculturalism. Solidarity is something that is nurtured and grown in the yearning for and living out of justice. Solidarity comes from hard work: listening, hearing, analyzing, questioning, rethinking, accepting, rejecting. It comes from a place of respecting and being respected.

This, I believe, does not come easily or naturally for most of us. If it were so natural, then we wouldn't be in the fix we are trying to get out of. To respect others means we must also respect ourselves. Centuries of inherited messages about the inherent evil of humanity (with a large measure of this brutalizing porridge aimed at women) pose a wall of judgment and condemnation that is hard for many of us to scale. As we seek to work together, we must always be working on ourselves. Perhaps this is where the comforting begins, as each of us has that dawning and then awakening in us: the point is *not* some religious version of perfection. Rather, we *live* our humanity with passion and vigor—regardless. We live our lives in justice and hope and even love—relentlessly. We recognize that none of us has a corner on righteousness, but that we are the ones we have been waiting for and, ultimately, there is no one to do this work for us.

This, then, is the first light of empowerment: when we realize that we cannot do the work of justice to end structural evil by individual acts of valor and conviction alone. They may help, to be sure, but tackling structural evil takes a whole bunch of folks with varieties of skills and insights.

This is because structures of domination rarely come in such pristine forms as circles, triangles, rectangles, or rhomboids. Structures of domination are like demonic ink blots. They have cores but their splatter marks are far and wide and absolutely dangerous: they can cause so much collateral damage that they disfigure and maim.

To speak of solidarity, to conjure standing *anywhere* together is to tempt the agony of the absurd. But frankly, I simply don't know what else to do and remain faithful to the gospel. Although Jordan's description of tinkering, daydreaming, revising, and memorizing does not sit well for this womanist ethicist, I do believe in strategizing, envisioning, challenging, debunking, and transforming. But this is always with an eye to sharing and receiving the dignity and gift of humanity and creation.

This means that a solidarity seeking the status quo is not one I can embrace. A solidarity that teaches a studied silence that rewards blind, thoughtless, clueless obedience and punishes vital curiosity is not one that I can come near. A solidarity that argues its "get tough on Iraq" case—one I agreed was needed because Saddam Hussein consistently and persistently showed himself to be a man willing to get what he wants at all costs, human and otherwise—but argues this case by making assertions about a nuclear program based on flawed or faked evidence is not one I believe we should wave this nation's flag over. A solidarity that is cobbled together with assertions about a link to Al Qaeda that people inside the intelligence services regard as nonsense—yet are largely unreported by our domestic news media so that most Americans have no idea why the rest of the world doesn't trust the Bush administration's motives—is not a solidarity that will hold from the center. A solidarity that denounces any criticism as unpatriotic is not one that is either patriotic or democratic. A solidarity that is forged on unchallenged and unsubstantiated claims without paying a price when those claims prove false; a solidarity coupled with saber rattling that gains it votes and silences opposition is one that will eventually destroy us as a nation *and* as people of faith.

Solidarity that only tolerates oppositional knowledge on playgrounds and streets, in homes and popular culture—but never in board meetings, religious councils, strategy sessions, policy development initiatives, pulpits, or curriculum revisions—is not a solidarity that is actually concerned about justice. It does not deserve my time, but it does need to be watched, monitored, like a hawk, and if necessary, be destroyed.

Whatever wisdom I have on solidarity and multiculturalism has been crafted from the hard experiences of learning over and over again that just because folk espouse solidarity does not mean they either know it or mean it. There are *many* good works being done to bring in justice, but there is only *one* of me. I must, as each of us must, make some choices about who I stand in solidarity with and how I will or will not deal with the differences that can enrich me, challenge me, deny me, destroy me. All of us must remember that we must not take so long to choose that our indecision or inaction makes the choice for us. We may choose wisely or foolishly, but the point is that we develop the ability to recognize where our actions are leading us and where we have actually gone. Then we can reformulate and assess on a continual basis whether we are truly working for justice or whether we have fallen into cooptation or complicity or betrayal.

There are *always* options—I've learned this from the trickster tradition in my culture. However, options cut both ways and sometimes even slice and dice. To move beyond the tight circle that we often seem caught in—one that is hollowed out by conservatism and liberalism—we must stop collapsing difference and diversity and plurality and multiculturalism and all such terms into such neat, antiseptic buzzwords. Instead, we must realize that we will not always agree. There will be times of reasoned (and unreasoned) dissent. We may *not* be able to work together on everything or every issue. Sometimes we must revise the rules we've learned through the years, or even as small children: the police are *not* always your friend, it is *not* always wise to wait to cross at a corner—or even to cross only at corners. In other words, there are few absolutes in life. Solidarities and multiculturalisms are just as caught up in this reality as episodes or steady diets of disaster and ruin.

As I continue being a part of growing Topsy, I do not sweat and summon whatever best there is in me to rescue the killers. I do try to give all of who I am to the work for justice and to hang in there with others who recognize that solidarities and differences are messy and utterly human. In some small way, this marks our humanity and turns the absurdities into living, breathing, and active hope.

chapter 5

Keeping the Dream Alive

Dwight N. Hopkins

——

Martin Luther King Jr. is recognized as one of the greatest United States citizens, not only in this country but around the world. He has become synonymous with faith, love, justice, compassion, sacrifice, and witnessing on behalf and with those who struggle to benefit from the opportunities of America. In a very interesting way, the social context in which he lived and died parallel this season of profound crisis and uncertainty both in the United States and on the global stage. King was deeply involved in the Civil Rights Movement, a valiant effort to provide basic guarantees of liberty for U.S. citizens. In particular, he stood for the civil rights of black Americans who for too long had been relegated to the ranks of second-class citizen in a land where they had helped produced the wealth for elite families during the period of slavery.[1]

So too, today, we find both an attack on civil rights and a groundswell to sustain the movement's gains and advance them further. We only have to note the uproar around the University of Michigan's policy on affirmative action.[2] I would submit that what is at stake here, just as it was in King's time, is not simply the admission of a few more black, brown, red, and yellow students. No, what is at stake is an entire philosophy of what America should be for all of its peoples. One philosophy holds that the nation should go back to a culture of rigid racial and ethnic asymmetry, similar to the period of slavery or at least like the period of de jure segregation. Another philosophy holds that, given the great mixture of different races and ethnic groups within the borders of this country, America can become a beacon for racial equality, mutual learning, and harmonious living regardless of the color of one's skin.

Furthermore, in addition to the racial and ethnic dimensions of civil rights for us today, we are also facing other civil rights issues. The gains of women are under pressure. There is still a glass ceiling for women. There is still a discrepancy between what women earn and what men earn. This is still a culture in which correct "family values" means that women and daughters automatically play a secondary role in the family, or that their only primary role is in the domestic sphere.

Civil rights for lesbians and gays have not even materialized—so it's not a question of going back to an even more retrograde era. This movement to recognize the rights of these American citizens has not really started. And an additional civil rights issue for us concerns one of the most egregiously regressive moves on the part of the U.S. government: the Patriot Act. Basically this bill states that the American people don't have any civil rights. So, like King, we face a challenge and an opportunity in the area of civil rights.

Dr. King, moreover, operated in a context in which poverty in America was so bad that the nation had to declare a national war on poverty. I would argue that we are dealing with a similar phenomenon today. This time, however, instead of the federal government declaring a war on poverty, the federal government and the very small handful of families that privately own the majority of the country's wealth have declared a war against those American citizens who are poor—a huge percentage being white workers and white people living in structural poverty. We are experiencing major layoffs of working-class people. The news media often spend a great deal of time covering the downsizing in corporate America as it pertains to white-collar management. But we could double or triple the firing of white working-class Americans and workers of color and see little media attention at all. To add insult to injury, federal and state governments are slashing safety net programs that in the past were taken for granted. There has been a radical shift in the country's culture and psyche: a citizen no longer has an obligation to help those who are worst off. There has been a further shift in the ideology in the federal government: the government should not use our tax monies to help the poor; instead the needs of the poor should be taken care of by the private sector, faith-based initiatives, or, in the worst-case scenario, the national government simply allows the poor to become poorer. However, just as there is a downward spiral for those dwelling in structural poverty, there is a simultaneous redistribution of wealth upward in the United States. Similarly, the federal government is still playing a role in issues of poverty and wealth, but this time it is providing increased tax breaks for the rich and huge, lucrative governmental contracts to wealthy monopoly capitalist corporations.

For King, the erosion of citizens' rights and the war against the poor were not the end of his theological concerns. From April 4, 1967, when he delivered his famous speech entitled "Beyond Vietnam," until his assassination on April 4, 1968, Dr. King added his ethical challenge against the war in Vietnam. And, again, we are living in a similar context today. The U.S. government and the handful of wealthy arms and oil corporations and "reconstruction businesses" who are the primary beneficiaries of the U.S. colonial occupations in Iraq and Afghanistan—an elite political and economic leadership who also have assigned young American men and women to the possibility and reality of death—these prosecutors and beneficiaries of the war have reoriented our priorities to such an extent that the billion dollars demanded for the dropping of bombs on Baghdad seems more important than using 850 billion dollars for eradicating poverty and racial inequality here in the United States. And 850 billion is the floor of the expense estimate, not the ceiling.

Like King, we too are confronted by times of crisis. Yet times of crisis always offer us opportunity for growth and healthy change. This is the good news. Fortunately, just as there were movements of resistance for a healthy America during Dr. King's time, we too have what I like to call a new American movement. And I think that high school and university students, as in the 1960s, are leading the way. In addition, many working-class people and their unions have opposed the war. E-mail and the Web have also been turned into sites for healthy debate and information exchange.

Marching, petition signing, writing to Congress, the building of various new organizations and ad hoc groups, increased conversations about international law, challenging public officials on their war records, signs of solidarity between the Americans and the people of Iraq, the recognition that the war budget means decreased spending on healthy domestic priorities, national and local efforts to influence public opinion, and the Supreme Court's deliberations on affirmative action—all of these and more are signs of hope. Yet in the midst of this flowering of resistance against and debates about civil rights, poverty, and war, a glaring question begs for a response. Where are the churches, where are the church leaders, where are the Christian institutions of higher learning, where are those who we naturally turn to for moral leadership in times of crisis? Dr. King offered us some instructive insight about the role of the church and Christian community during situations of crisis and opportunity.

First, for King, the Christian church must be a beacon for justice. If Christians dared to witness as followers of Jesus the Christ, then we would have to practice what Jesus practiced and preached. From King's vantage point, justice stood at the heart of the cross and resurrection; it stood at the heart of Christian suffering, hope, and love. Those persons of any color or ethnicity who claimed the name of Jesus deserved that name only if they anchored their Christian faith and identity in justice. As he wrote in 1957, the "belief that God is on the side of truth and justice comes down to us from the long tradition of our Christian faith."[3]

Accordingly, the church could not be a Christian family if it supported a racial hierarchy, or a U.S. military presence abroad, or a decline in civil rights. And most definitely, King argued, no church could identify itself as Christian if it supported the wealthy over the poor. Maybe people could call themselves a gathering of like-minded individuals, or a group of people interested in religion. But until black, brown, red, yellow, and white Americans placed truth and justice at the center of their faith, then and only then could a people of faith claim themselves believers in and doers of Jesus's words and deeds.

A Christian church of justice, from King's perspective, would emerge once the church de-emphasized such activities as fund-raising for the pastor's anniversary or expanding church facilities merely to clam bragging rights. Justice would not be found in those churches where pastors paid more attention to the "size of their wheelbase" than to righting incorrect relations outside church walls.[4] To really have church, he believed, called for centering worship and witness around efforts for justice.

Second, a Christian church distinguishes itself through the role of servant. Justice manifests itself through active service for those who suffer from physical poverty and need, those who are emotionally broken, those who cannot advocate for themselves, and those who lack full human dignity. Toward the end of his life, King summed up all that he has done and asked that his eulogy convey the following message: "I don't want a long funeral. . . . But I hope I can live so well that the preacher can get up and say he was faithful. . . . That's the sermon I'd like to hear." Defining the nature of Christian faith by servanthood, he finishes:

> "Well done my good and faithful servant. You've been faithful; you've been concerned about others." That's where I want to go from this point on, the rest of my days. "He who is greatest among you shall be your servant." I want to be a servant. I want to be a witness for my Lord, do something for others.[5]

The nature of the Christian church does not define itself by worldly possessions and materialistic acquisitions. In fact, in the list of his own earthly achievements, King does not detail his Nobel Peace Prize, his many speaking and preaching engagements, his prestigious degrees, or his books and articles. In contrast, he hopes the living will remember him for his lifelong service to the physically poor and to society's powerless victims. Again, the nature of the church is to serve and empower the people, even if (in the case of exceedingly wealthy churches) serving implies sharing power equally with the poor.

King based the servant trait of the Christian church on the Bible. Specifically, he refers to the passage beginning at Matthew 25:31. Here Jesus uses the parable about the ultimate judgment day, when specific criteria deny or permit passage into heaven. All of humankind faces Jesus on the throne and awaits either permission to enter eternal life or relegation to hell or prolonged condemnation. On the left, Jesus places the goats—those who pursued an earthly lifestyle of materialistic, profit-oriented activity. In this crowd one discovers those who placed profit before people, the value of things above human value. Here, too, one meets all those so-called Christians who preached an abstract "spiritual" religion, which primarily encouraged individuals to gaze at the heavens while systems of greed, racism, and war enslaved the spirits, souls, and bodies of victims on earth.

On the right hand, Jesus places all the sheep and gives them access to heaven because they had been faithful servants to the world's physically poor: people without food to eat or water to drink, people incarcerated or homeless, people sick or without clothes, immigrants to a strange land. King wanted the Christian church to stand with the sheep. As Jesus states in the parable: "Verily I say unto you, inasmuch as ye have done it unto one of the least of these my brethren, ye have done it unto me" (Matt. 25:40). What the Christian church does to society's poor equals what is done to Jesus Christ.

Third, the church obtains its Christian identity when it organizes for the God-given rights of the poor. Specifically, what the church organizes for is not the esthetic and romantic notion of integration. For King, the Christian church fights to realize a new definition of equality in which power-sharing would satisfy the new understanding of racial and ethnic integration. In other words, racial integration, which King continued to pursue, would arise only when what he called the white power structure surrendered its exclusive monopoly on power.

Clarifying the goal of Christian organizing efforts, Dr. King lectured in 1967: "Now, if we are to recognize that we are in this new era where the struggle is for genuine equality, we must recognize that we can't solve our problems until there is a radical redistribution of economic and political power." Furthermore, the new power that the poor and the black community would receive in "genuine equality" would reflect the natural rights given by God in God's focus on the poor. Continuing, he asserted: "We must recognize that if we are to gain our God-given rights now, principalities and powers must be confronted and they must be changed."[6]

Basically King wanted to clarify the organizing target of the Christian religion and the church and thus facilitate a full humanity for all people. Christians must sharpen their tools of social analysis and clearly identify and confront the "principalities and powers" on earth that block the achievement of oppressed peoples' God-given rights. Toward the end of his life, King began to define these demonic powers as racism, capitalism, and capitalist war abroad. He held that to enjoy the rights freely given through God's grace entails eradicating systemic evil. To organize toward what it means to be human forces the church to name immoral activities. Naming evil, then, comprises part of the organizing effort; fully removing it helps restore just human relations, a new and equal power-sharing.

Finally, the church has to heal, preach, and help deliver. Here, King uses Luke 4:18-19 as his personal guide and, by implication, as instruction for all Christian witness. Not only does the church define itself by justice, servanthood, and organizing, but it also heals those who have broken hearts. At this point King adds a concern for the soul, which encompasses the heart. Just as the physical body needs material sustenance, the soul and the heart likewise require care. Therefore Christians provide relief for the nonmaterial while challenging systemic principalities and powers.

Related to healing is the proclamation of the gospel message, or good news, for those who are poor. As a fourth-generation Baptist preacher, King knew all too well the importance of the proclaimed word in the Christian faith tradition. The people need to hear a word from the Lord to soothe their souls, direct their vision, gird up their courage to confront and change systems of evil, and assume their God-given rights in the here and now.

In particular the proclaimed word tells society's poor and afflicted that "the acceptable year of the Lord" is at hand, not tomorrow but now. In fact, the year most acceptable to a God of justice and truth was the year of Jubilee, when all slaves received their deliverance into freedom. Consequently, the church must help in this deliverance by letting society's victims hear that a radical transformation has already occurred with the birth, life, death, and resurrection of Jesus the Christ.

Specifically, the coming of Jesus meant deliverance from evil had taken place. If deliverance into the realm of Jesus's own liberation has occurred for the poor, then the church must aid the poor in their own deliverance. Put differently, Jesus shifted the balance of power from the realm of evil to the realm of freedom, thereby making victory of the oppressed assured. Though a historical shift has taken place in terms of guaranteeing Jesus's victory for "the little ones" on earth, the victims must allow this already ultimate deliverance to empower them toward making this liberation concrete. The Christian church has a role in this process; it proclaims and helps organize deliverance.[7]

In addition, Martin Luther King Jr. offers us some insight about the nature of spirituality. He does this by standing in a specific spiritual tradition when, on another occasion, he paraphrases once again Luke 4:18 and proclaims: "Jesus said the spirit of the Lord is upon me, because he's anointed me to heal the broken hearted, to preach the gospel to the poor, to bring deliverance to those who are in captivity and to proclaim the acceptable year of the Lord. And I must confess that the spirit of the Lord is upon me."[8] Here, in his biblical interpretation, King stresses two aspects of a theological spirituality.

The first act of Christian spirituality is not correct doctrine, but a freeing service to the poor, the homeless, the unemployed, those victims of AIDS and rape, the immigrant stranger, the hungry, and those without proper clothing. Christian spirituality means confronting the everyday pain and humiliation that confront the faceless in society. It means commitment to and standing with those who suffer. To be compelled by the Spirit, then, the church has to root itself, primarily, in the communities and neighborhoods of poor whites and people of color where, from King's perspective, the Lord's spirit was born and still resides. Christian spirituality greets the church in the struggle for freedom of the least of these in society: "The truth will set you free" (John 8:32). Indeed, for the spirituality of the eleven o'clock black church service on Sunday to be authenticated, this Sunday spirituality has to receive God's presence in suffering and struggle in the Monday through Saturday lower income communities of North America. It is this latter spirit that "will guide you into all the truth" (John 16:13).

The practice of a theological spirituality fundamentally means social transformation of the harmful structures and systems that push down the most vulnerable people in the United States. Any talk about the Spirit in the church that leaves a satanic systemic spirit in place serves the injustice that breeds a harmful form of capitalism, second-class status for women, a military presence abroad, oppression of those with same-gender attractions, and, of course, white supremacy over African Americans and other people of color.

Moreover, the anointing of "the spirit of the Lord" commissions us to proclaim the good news of freedom. God's loving freedom has become our freedom because Jesus's victory over oppression has opened up a new world where everlasting life begins now (John 3:16). This spirit calls on theology to speak with, for, and to those who have no voices. It calls on theology to say the gospel of freedom for a full individual and collective life reigns now for our fellow citizens who need our help and, in fact, for our fellow citizens around the entire globe. Martin Luther King Jr. recognized the prophetic nature of speaking the truth about Christian spiritual anointing: "We are called," King proclaimed, "to speak for the weak, for the voiceless, for the victims of our nation."[9]

The poor have to hear that Jesus's goals have won and, therefore, have made them somebody. The "somebodiness" of the proclaimed gospel is not a mushy, feel-good, hedonistic self-indulgence. It, on the contrary, empowers the poor to realize their true spiritual identity. For the African American poor in particular it affirms their African self identity. Part of announcing a liberating spirituality to the black victims of society, then, is to tell them that their African self or their black self comes from the grace of God. This is why Dr. King at one point shouted out loud: "Yes, we must stand up and say, 'I'm black and I'm beautiful', and this self affirmation is the black man's need, made compelling by the white man's crimes against him."[10] The self-identity language of blackness and Africanness has the potential to grip the poor and help them to see, with new eyes, the reality and future possibilities of a new heaven on earth. If the social and language structures of the dominating white society have been subverted by the good news of the vision and goals of Jesus, then poor black people no longer feel defined by a white ruling culture. They claim and name themselves in the liberated space created by Jesus's liberating spirit. To say who you are is part of waging war against egregious labels that deny your humanity. Culture (that is, the act of identifying oneself in accordance with freedom), then, is an important aspect of black theology's transformative spirituality.

Coupled with suggesting the need to revisit and broaden our vision of healthy spirituality, King's life and theology urge us to consider seriously the Christian necessity and the risks of faith when we oppose the U.S. government and its thirst for oil in foreign lands.

On April 4, 1967, at the Riverside Church in New York City, exactly one year before his martyrdom, Martin Luther King Jr. gave his classic "Beyond Vietnam" speech. Immediately after this historic Christian witness, Dr. King was opposed by the president of the United States, the FBI, many other national civil rights leaders, foundation funding sources, the white-controlled mainstream press, several board members of his own organization (the Southern Christian Leadership Conference, or SCLC), and thousands of Americans across the land. He was instructed that the black church should stick to domestic issues like race, or winning souls to Christ, or hooping and tuning. He was told that the black church should not mix international issues with domestic issues. Despite these condescending instructions and lethal threats, King believed that failure to speak out when the United States government goes to war against a smaller nation would be a prime instance when silence meant betrayal: not betrayal of the United States but betrayal of the gospel of Jesus Christ. In a situation of superpower aggression, opposition to the thirst for oil through war is the best example of black homiletical hooping and tuning.

As an ordained Christian pastor, King could not separate the

Lordship of Christ from the rest of reality. He viewed all of reality as interconnected. That is why he wrote the following:

> Now when I say question the whole of society, it means ultimately coming to the see that the problem of racism, the problem of economic exploitation, and the problem of war are all tied together. . . .
>
> A nation that will keep people in slavery for 244 years will "thingify" them, make them things. Therefore they will exploit them, and poor people generally, economically. And a nation that will exploit economically will have to have foreign investments and everything else, and will have to use its military might to protect them. All of these problems are tied together.[11]

What King teaches us is that there is a direct connection between the U.S. government's actions as a global superpower on the one hand, and, on the other hand, its negative domestic policies. The same forces that benefitted from a structure of white power and a redistribution of wealth upward inside of the United States were the exact same forces that demonized people of color in the Third World and made plans to steal their oil outside of the United States. In a similar way, monies set aside for poor folk and working-class families domestically will now be used to pay monopoly capitalist corporations that make products for war internationally. All one has to do is ask a series of questions: How much does one bomb cost? How much do aircraft cost? How much does a naval carrier cost? Who makes these machines for killing people in other lands? Are they owned by the collective American people or by a small handful of families? After the United States invades Third World countries and takes their oil, does the ownership of that oil go into the collective hands of the American people or into the private hands of a small group of families? These are the types of questions that Dr. King was posing when he spoke out against the Vietnam War. In response, he was labeled unpatriotic, a communist sympathizer, and a supporter of terrorism. But King would not compromise the gospel of Christ; that is why he called the U.S. government the "greatest purveyor of violence in the world today."[12] In King's eyes, war abroad meant economic and spiritual death for the disadvantaged within the borders of the United States. He makes this comment: "Here we spend thirty-five billion dollars a year to fight this terrible war in Vietnam and just the other day the Congress refused to vote forty-four million to get rid of rats in the slums and the ghettos of our country."[13]

The United States government's acts of violence through war in the Third World were not simply accidents or aberrations from the normal activities of the federal administration and the monopoly corporations that it served. Employing a systemic social analysis of the international situation, Dr. King thought it was logical that the federal government was "the greatest purveyor of violence in the world today." For King, the imperial war conducted by a super-power against poor nations of color mirrored the same domestic capitalist war against poor white people and people of color. To fight against racial discrimination and against the poverty faced by white Americans at home automatically led into a global struggle. Consequently King preached: "I have said that the problem, the crisis we face, is international in scope. In fact, it is inseparable from an international emergency which involves the poor, the dis-possessed, and the exploited of the whole world."[14]

Not only was the United States government the greatest initia-tor of global violence on the face of the earth, it was also one of the main, if not the primary, economic investors that stole natural resources from and exploited cheap labor in the Third World. A vast unequal exchange existed between the actual value of raw materials and people of color's physical labor in Africa, Asia, the Caribbean, Latin America, and the Pacific Islands, on the one hand, and the wages they received and the compensation obtained for wealth stolen from their underdeveloped countries, on the other hand. In other words, the U.S. government and the elite monopoly capitalist corporations that support it were using the military, direct investments, and control of international financial organizations to reap billions of dollars from the cheap labor of working-class people in the Third World. In the context of calling for a "true revolution of values," Dr. King linked the demonic nature of capitalism and its foreign investments when he stated:

> A true revolution of values will soon look uneasily on the glaring contrast of poverty and wealth. With righteous indignation, it will look across the seas and see individual capitalists of the West investing huge sums of money in Asia, Africa and South America, only to take the profits out with no concern for the social betterment of [these] countries.[15]

Indeed, from Dr. King's analysis, the countries of the Third World became underdeveloped precisely from a conscious political policy on the part of the United States government, the military-industrial machinery, and the elite group of billionaire corporations that sucked Third World countries dry. When King surveyed the international scene, he saw a vast discrepancy between the poverty in Third World countries and the enormous wealth accumulated by Western powers. Monopoly capitalism does not stop at pushing down racial minorities and white working-class people at home; it also needs capital transfusions and consumer markets abroad.

Moreover, Dr. King understood the marriage between United States violence abroad and unjust economic investments: "We in the West must bear in mind that the poor countries are poor primarily because we have exploited them through political and economic colonialism. Americans in particular must help their nation repent of her modern economic imperialism."[16] King teaches us that the conscience of an "awakened activist" cannot remain satisfied with a shortsighted focus on local problems, if only because she or he "sees that local problems are all interconnected with world problems."[17]

And if one bears the cross of Christ, one has to assume politically a systemic analysis of international relations because injustice and evil at home will never cease until injustice and evil abroad cease. To limit our vision only to the rough waves of domestic race relations and poverty would be like seeing only Jesus's baptism in the calmness of the river Jordan but not comprehend the Christian mandate that we must walk also with him on the rough seas of Galilee throughout the world.

Likewise King opposed U.S. wars abroad because he felt that he was called to be consistently nonviolent. As a pastor of a local church and a recipient of the Nobel Peace Prize, he felt compelled to counsel against the use of violence not only in the Civil Rights Movement; he also believed that killing people at home or abroad was wrong. For him, nonviolence was not a political tactic or a lesson in a manual on civil disobedience. Nonviolence was a personal and theological way of life for him. That is why he wrote about the government and the media:

> They applauded us in the sit-in movement when we nonviolently decided to sit in at lunch counters. They applauded us on the freedom rides when we accepted blows without retaliation. They praised us in . . . Birmingham and Selma, Alabama. Oh, the press was so noble in its applause and . . . praise when I would say "Be nonviolent toward Bull Connor." . . . "Be nonviolent toward Jim Clark." There is something strangely inconsistent about a nation and a press that would praise you when you say, "Be nonviolent toward Jim Clark," but will curse and damn you when you say, "Be nonviolent toward little brown Vietnamese children!"[18]

The Rev. Dr. Martin Luther King Jr. exemplifies the tough choices for the clergy and lay leadership of the church of Jesus Christ. His profound sense of justice for the disadvantaged and those cast aside in the marketplace of life, his consistent focus on starting all of his ministry with the plight of the poor, and his sober imitation of Jesus's call to love one's enemy are all being sorely tested today. In today's society where pulpits spew the prosperity gospel, where too many churches spend hardly any time on poor babies after they are born and most of their preaching on "the right to life," where it is fashionable for ministers to either support or take a "wait and see" attitude in the nation's current war over oil, King sounds like a voice crying in the wilderness. Yet if we are to take seriously the importance of racial justice (and, of course, gender justice), then like King we must take on race, gender, poverty, and war as an integrated whole. The key is a justice based on love. It is the underlying thread that holds together all that we do—whether it is in our families, churches, communities, nation, or the world. Love is that thread. However, as we close with King's words, we see that it is a tough love. Dr. King preached:

> Could it be that [people] do not know that the good news was meant for all men [and women]—for Communist and capitalist, for their children and ours, for black and for white, for revolutionary and conservative? Have they forgotten that my ministry is in obedience to the one who loved his enemies so fully that he died for them? What then can I say to the "Vietcong" or to Castro or to Mao as a faithful minister of this one? Can I threaten them with death or must I not share with them my life?[19]

I hope my sharing with you, in this essay, some reflections on Martin Luther King Jr. as a window into the relationships among black theology, the black church, and the contemporary experience—I hope this sharing will prompt you to do some critical reflection and self-reflection on the nature of your faith. I trust that these remarks have provided some food for thought and further discussion.

chapter 6

The Dream

A Future for the Present

Justo L. González

——◅

I met Dr. Martin Luther King Jr. on February 17, 1962. It was in Puerto Rico during my very first year of teaching. He had been invited to Puerto Rico by the Fellowship of Reconciliation (FOR) and, simply because I had some friends in the FOR, I had been assigned to be the interpreter for his speeches. It was no easy task, translating for a man whose words cascaded in an avalanche of eloquence, and I confess that I failed miserably! Still, I would not exchange that failure for any subsequent success, for if I was not able to capture his eloquence, his dream was certainly able to captivate me.

The "I Have a Dream" speech was still in the future. But the dream was clearly there. It was a vast and valiant dream, one that dared see beyond the racism that had always engulfed his life. It was a very realistic dream, one that began by acknowledging that everything was stacked against it. In between Dr. King's various commitments, we had several conversations I shall never forget. He was staying at the seminary where I was teaching, next door to my apartment. In my living room, which was also my study, we talked about slavery, and Jim Crow, and lynchings, and the KKK. He spoke of all these things as very real and very powerful, yet he also spoke of them as enemies that did not stand a chance against truth and right. At that point it dawned on me that his dream was not just a dream. It was a vision of the future—a vision one could join or ignore or resist, but never undo.

Then the conversation drifted to other subjects. We talked about the poverty he had seen in Puerto Rico, and about the difference between that and the poverty of Puerto Ricans in New York. We talked about poverty in the United States, and about its complex relationship with race and racism. It was the time when the nation was becoming increasingly entangled in Vietnam. Just a few months before I had been unable to return to my own motherland in Cuba because of political circumstances there, so I was very much inclined to accept the official line: that what was happening in Vietnam was one more case of democracy resisting communist aggression. It was Dr. King who first showed me the fallacies in such an argument.

As I now look back on those conversations in the light of Dr. King's later career, I realize that I was being told that the dream was much vaster than I had imagined, that the struggle was much greater than the news media recognized. The dream was not just about a much-deserved vindication for the enslaved African people of North America. The dream was also about the liberation of all enslaved and oppressed people everywhere. The dream was not only about the right to sit where others sat, to eat where others ate, and to study where others studied. The dream was also about the right of every human being to be treated as such, to be respected as such, to be loved as such. The dream was about justice, about justice for all, about a justice that would embrace peace and be grounded in love.

That is why the dream has taken hold of other dreamers throughout the world and has broken forth into a multitude of similar dreams. That is why when Puerto Ricans now march against the U.S. Navy's use of the island of Vieques for target practice, they sing *Vamos a vencer*—"We shall overcome." That is why, when I asked a group of seminary students in the People's Republic of China who they thought represented the best of American culture, their almost unanimous response was "Dr. Martin Luther King Jr." The dream is now a worldwide dream, one that encompasses many races, many cultures, many religions, many wrongs that need to be righted.

Here in this country, forty years later, we look back to the "I Have a Dream" speech as a defining moment in the history of the nation. And so we celebrate its fortieth anniversary. Yet many look back to that moment with heavy hearts and perplexed minds. What happened to the dream? Where did we go wrong? Certainly many gains have been made. Laws have been passed. Official segregation has been outlawed. Schools, businesses, and churches have cracked the door open. But there is still so far to go! There is still an unholy relationship between race and poverty, between race and incarceration, between race and underschooling, between race and premature death.

To make matters worse, some who got in through the crack in the door are doing little to open the door wider, and even less to change the building.

And, to make matters even more perplexing, while in 1963 there was much justification for thinking of racial issues in this country as essentially bipolar—black and white—today the matter has become much more complex, with the presence and the claims of a multiplicity of races and cultures all demanding recognition and space, all mixing and mingling in an ever-changing kaleidoscope.

This leads me back to my conversations with Dr. King so many years ago, and to my thoughts about those conversations some time later, as I watched him on television delivering his epoch-making speech. I remember being inspired and overwhelmed, as so many of us have been time and again, by the power of that speech. I remember admiring the oratory of Dr. King, with its inimitable cadences and its captivating imagery—an oratory I had been unable to translate adequately some years back. But that was not the ultimate reason for the power of the speech, or for the power of the dream. I remember thinking also of the authority of the man, of the struggles he had led, of all that he had suffered and accomplished. That too was awesome. Yet even that was not the ultimate reason for the power of the dream. I remember thinking of the generations of suffering and exploited Africans brought to these shores, whose ghosts now stood behind him at that podium, and the overwhelming justice of their cause. But even that was not the ultimate reason for the power of the dream.

The dream had power because it was not just a dream. It was not the wishful thinking of a man dreaming of a better time or a better place, no matter how eloquent the man or how just his cause. The dream had power because it was not just a dream, but a vision. It was a vision of the way things were meant to be. It was the certainty that because this is the way things are meant to be, that is the way they shall be.

A dream shatters when one wakes up, broken by the painful realities of the present world. A vision takes place in the midst of those realities, and yet acknowledges an even more powerful reality. A vision is a glimpse of the future so clear, so certain, that one can stake life on it.

And therein lies the power of Dr. King's dream. It is not just a dream. It is also a vision. It is akin to the vision of the prophet of old: "They shall beat their swords into plowshares, and their spears into pruning hooks; nation shall not lift up sword against nation, neither shall they learn war any more; but they shall sit under their own vines and under their own fig trees, and no one shall make them afraid; for the mouth of the Lord has spoken" (Mic. 4:3-4). It is akin to the vision of the exile on Patmos: "After this I looked, and there was a great multitude that no one could count, from every nation, from all tribes and peoples and languages, standing before the throne and before the Lamb, robed in white, with palm branches on their hands" (Rev. 7:9). It is a vision grounded of the promise of the One whom we call Lord of lords: "People will come from east and west, from north and south, and will sit at the table in the kingdom of God. Indeed, some are last who will be first, and some are first who will be last" (Luke 13:29-30).

Therein lies the ultimate power of the dream. It is not just Dr. King's dream. It is the promise of the One who is "the true one . . . who opens and no one will shut, who shuts and no one will open" (Rev. 3:7). When we speak of Dr. King's vision, we are not just dealing with a dream that was good for the 1960s, but is now a matter of past history. Those who took it as a mere dream may no longer follow it. Some will forsake it for other dreams—for dreams of individual success or of personal status. Others will forsake it because it is not reflected in the nightmarish realities of the ghetto, where it is so difficult to dream. Some will simply decide that the world has changed, that today's issues are different from those of the 1960s, and that it is now time to move on to something else.

But if the dream is more than a dream, if the dream is a vision of God's purposes for humankind, if the dream, more than a great man's speech, reflects the speech of the God who says "Let there be," and there is, then nothing can undo it. For as another prophet said in another time, "Though this world with devils filled should threaten to undo us"—though this world, filled with prejudice, and inequity, and violence, and oppression, should threaten to undo the vision—"we will not fear, for God has willed God's truth to triumph." And *that* no devil, no oppression, no present-day devil, can ever undo.

It is important for us to remember this, because, as in this book's title, the "dream" and the "future" belong together. We are not speaking of a dream that is past and a future that is to come. We are speaking rather of a future that makes itself present to us by means of a dream, a vision. The vision itself is the powerful presence of the future among us, laying bare our sin and our injustice, and at the very same time, as an act of grace, as Gospel breaking through Law, reassuring us that sin and injustice will not have the last word.

Thus let us return to our title: *I Have a Dream: Martin Luther King Jr. and the Future of Multicultural America.*

As we consider this theme, it is important to note that we are not speaking of a future multicultural America. We are speaking of the future of a multicultural America that is already here. The question is not, will America become multicultural? The question is rather, what will become of an America that is already multicultural? (And let me hasten to add: the very fact that I agreed to contribute to such a title is already a sign of some of the demands of the present multicultural reality. I find it very strange and even preposterous that a single nation dares usurp the name of an entire hemisphere and call itself "America," as if the rest did not exist or had no claim on what is in fact a common name. So for me to speak of "multicultural America," when what in fact is meant is "multicultural United States," is already a sort of concession to multiculturalism. Therefore, since multiculturalism demands that we all make some concessions, throughout this presentation I shall abide by the terms of the title, and say "America" when in fact I mean the United States, and I shall say "American" when in fact I mean "United-Statesian"!)

America is already a multicultural society. At least it is a place where many cultures meet and mingle. The fact is so obvious that it needs no proof, for we all see it in everyday life. Thirty years ago, when I first moved to Atlanta, I had to look in the phone book to find other people who spoke Spanish. Today all I have to do is go to the nearest mall to hear people speaking Spanish all over the place, and Arabic, and Tamil, and Russian, and Swahili, and Korean, and Chinese. Thus, once again, the question is not whether the future of America will be multicultural, but rather, what will the future be for an America that is already multicultural, even though many Americans do not recognize it as such?

But let us not hasten to rejoice in this present multicultural reality without acknowledging the evil it reflects. America is a multicultural reality because the Europeans who conquered these lands—mostly British along the East Coast, and Spanish in the West and Southwest—did not find these lands unoccupied. Therefore America first became multicultural through a massive land grab. Then, relating more directly to the issues that were close at hand for Dr. Martin Luther King Jr., America became multicultural through a genocidal importation of slave labor from Africa. And then, just as the national conscience was being aroused to the injustices and the crime of slavery, America became even more multicultural by grabbing half of the land belonging to Mexico. And what about the manner in which not only America but also many other parts of the world, particularly Europe, have become multicultural and multiethnic in recent decades?

There is a passage in the book of Revelation that deals directly with this matter. It is a passage often quoted, but seldom read in its socioeconomic context. In Revelation 17, John speaks of the great harlot, which clearly is the city of Rome, sitting on seven hills. The vision also refers to the "many waters" on which the harlot is seated. This is clearly an allusion to the wealth of Rome, for in ancient times most long-distance trade took place by means of water transport, and the image of a city sitting on water was frequently used to refer to its wealth. In this particular case, however, we are told more. The angel explains to John that "the waters that you saw, where the whore is seated, are peoples and multitudes and nations and languages." In other words, that Rome is rich because the wealth and the resources of all these many lands and peoples and languages have been made to flow towards it. I have tried to show elsewhere that the book of Revelation acutely evokes the evolving multicultural reality both of the Roman Empire and of the nascent Christian church.[1] John has much positive to say about how these many tribes, and nations, and languages are called into God's future. But he is also aware that the growing multicultural reality of Rome is not just the result of people moving because of mere curiosity or wanderlust. People come to Rome because the wealth of the nations flows to Rome.

Likewise, there is a connection between American wealth and the present American multicultural reality. This certainly is true of those foundational events I have already mentioned—the taking of the lands from the original inhabitants and later from Mexico, and the taking of labor and freedom from a significant portion of the population of Africa. But it is also true of more recent trends towards a more complex multicultural reality, both in America and elsewhere. Why have so many Africans moved to England, if not because over generations much of the wealth of England has been built on the exploitation of Africa? Why do the French have to guard their southern borders like a European Rio Grande, if not because over generations much of the wealth of France has been built on the exploitation of Northern Africa? Why are so many people trying to cross our own Rio Grande, if not because the inequity on the two sides of the border is such that it naturally seeks to level out? Indeed, the Mexican family that crosses illegally under the bridge is simply the other side of the same coin:

the carnations that cross legally over the bridge have been grown on the land where the Mexican family used to grow corn and beans. Why are there today so many Central Americans in the United States, if not because the exportation of cheap meat for fast-food restaurants in the United States has made land in much of Central America too valuable for peasants to own and cultivate for their own food? Where the rivers of wealth flow, there flow also the rivers of population, and there is no immigration reform, and no beefed-up border patrol, that can ever stem that flow. The Seer of Patmos had it right: the wealth of the centers of empire is built on many nations, and peoples, and languages, and just as the wealth of those many nations flows to the centers of Empire, so does the impoverished population of those nations flow in the same direction.

So a multicultural presence is not necessarily a good thing. It is not necessarily good in its origins, as the history I have just outlined clearly shows. And it is not necessarily good in its results, for multiculturalism often leads to exploitation of one group by another, as the same history also shows. Quite often a society may claim to be multicultural because it involves the presence of more than one culture. But also quite often one of those cultures claims dominion over the others, makes itself normative, and manages to make cultural differences into an excuse for oppression and exploitation.

It is not enough just to be multicultural. American society was multicultural before the Civil Rights Movement. But this was a patently unjust multiculturalism—indeed, it was a multicultural-ism where cultural and other differences between the dominant and the oppressed were used to justify the unjustifiable.

At this point, it is important to remember that Dr. King's dream was not only about the rights of an oppressed people. It was also about relationships. It was about black and white children playing together. It was about a society in which everyone's contribution would be accepted and appreciated. Therefore, if that dream is to become a reality in America's multicultural society, it cannot simply be a dream of a society where every culture will be allowed to exist, but rather of a society where the contribution of each culture will be accepted and valued.

This must be so, for cultures are not static realities. A culture is a system of artifacts, actions, and symbols that a particular group of people develop as they seek to respond to the challenges of their environment. While environment is not all that determines a culture, it certainly is an important factor in deciding the shape of a culture, and the way in which it will develop. The Aleuts of Alaska have developed a culture in response to the climatic conditions of the extreme North. The Quiché of Guatemala have developed another in response to their tropical conditions. When Quiché people move to Alaska—as many have done recently—there are many aspects of their traditional culture that they'll be able to keep. But there are others, such as clothing and housing patterns, that must evolve in response to the new environment. And the same would be true were a group of Aleuts to move from the Aleutian Islands to the Caribbean. Environment is an important factor in the way a culture develops.

Cultures are living realities. Like all living things, cultures must relate to their environment. They must breathe. They must be nourished. They must change their environment and be changed by it. A culture that needs to be preserved is on the way to extinction, just as a living being that has to be constantly protected from its environment is on the way to death. This means that a truly multicultural society, a society in which all cultures are allowed to flourish and to develop, must be also a society in which cultures interact, not simply one in which they exist side by side. In fact, examples could be given of past societies where a number of different cultures were allowed to exist side by side with the dominant culture, and eventually, rather than multicultural societies, they became graveyards of cultures.

I shall go further. Too often culture, and also race, is falsely objectified and turned into what it is not, in order to justify the goals or interests of those doing the defining. Let me begin with the issue of race. We tend to think that racism is the result of race, that somehow race is an objective reality that stands at the root of racism and racial discrimination. But the fact is that race is not such an objective reality. Rather it is a social construct, shaped and defined in order to serve other goals. Some time ago, someone asked a Haitian dictator what proportion of the population of Haiti was white. He responded: "About 90 percent." The American reporter who had asked the question demanded to know how that could be, since almost everyone he ever saw in Haiti was black. The Haitian's answer was: "You see, in the United States you count as black anyone who has a bit of black blood. Here, we count as white anyone who has a bit of white blood." When you stop to think about it, one of those definitions has about the same objective validity as the other. If in the United States people count as black when they are three-fourths of European descent and one-fourth African, the reason is not some objective reality, but simply the fact that for a number of reasons it has seemed convenient to those who set the society's cultural parameters to define race in a particular way.

Something that happened in California in the nineteenth century illuminates the point. When the territory had to report its number of white citizens in order to become a state, it was decided that Mexicans were white. A few years later, after statehood had been granted, a court decided that Mexicans could not perform certain functions as witnesses, because they were not white.[2] Thus, racism is not the result of race. On the contrary, race is the result of racism.

Certainly some people are more colorless than others. Some have rounder eyes than others. Some have yellow hair, and some have black. But in objective terms it is impossible to say where one "race" ends and another begins.

In some ways, the same is true of cultures. In this country and at the present time, I am fond of speaking about "Hispanics" or about "Latinos and Latinas." But the reality is much more complex than that, and much more resistant to easy classification. I grew up in Cuba, and my speech intonations in my native Spanish are very different from those of Mexico, or the Dominican Republic, or of Colombia, or of Argentina. In a way, each of those represents a different culture. Furthermore, when I was growing up in Cuba those of us from Havana and its surroundings used to make fun of those from the eastern end of the island, because they had a different intonation because they used a few different words, because they had some customs of their own—in other words, because they represented a different culture. Thus, if today in this country I choose to speak of "Hispanic culture," I do so not because there is an objective and uniform reality on which we all agree, but rather because I and others find it to our advantage to stand as one, and thus emphasize our common traits while underplaying our differences.

The same is true even of the dominant culture in this country. Sometimes we speak of it as one culture. But then I hear people commenting about "southern culture," and in the South I hear some people distinguishing between the culture of Appalachia and that of Mississippi.

In brief, cultures, like races, are social constructs. Certainly, there is a degree of objective justification for our various definitions of culture. Hispanics generally speak Spanish, and not Swahili or German. But still, cultures, like races, are defined and delimited according to the interests of those with the power to define.

For these reasons, it is important to clarify exactly what we mean by "multicultural"—in other words, what is the goal of the vision. It is clear that the old paradigm of America as a melting pot is no longer valid—if it ever was. For one thing, the supposed melting pot never allowed everyone to melt and mix with the rest, as the Civil Rights Movement and Dr. King's career amply show. The mix in the pot was open only to those whom the larger mass was willing to bring into its fold. Those whom the larger mass wished to keep out of the mix, so they could perform the lower functions in society, were never invited into the melting pot. And those who were allowed in were required to leave most of their distinctiveness behind, so that Germans, Swedes, and Italians were expected to forget the languages of their ancestors. But even though the melting-pot paradigm leaves much to be desired, it is important to recognize that it was a way to conceive a multicultural reality. Once again, it is not enough to be multicultural. It is important to recognize *how* we are multicultural.

Others have spoken of a multicultural society in terms of a mosaic in which each tile retains its distinctiveness, and the total picture must be perceived as a whole. This is better than the melting-pot paradigm, for it does not expect all cultures to disappear into one, and it does recognize that each of the various cultures in a multicultural situation has something to contribute to the whole.

But this also is an insufficient paradigm, for it looks upon cultures as fixed realities with clearly defined borders. In a mosaic, tiles remain distinct and do not influence each other. They are glued in place, and their mutual relationship is determined by the total picture. They are not free to change positions and relationships, to influence each other—in other words, to adapt and to grow.

Once again, cultures are like living organisms. They must take from their environment, and give to it, in order to survive. In that give and take, they evolve. It is precisely in this evolution that cultures show their vitality, as they prove themselves capable of responding to different and even unexpected challenges—sometimes challenges from the other cultures which they encounter.

Furthermore, the paradigm of the mosaic implies that cultures are objectively defined realities, and ignores the fact that cultures are social constructs whose definitions constantly change as the issues in society change, and as the various interests of those defining cultures evolve.

For these reasons, we need a more dynamic paradigm to help us understand the complex relationships among cultures as they encounter each other, and as they define and shape themselves as well as others. Along these lines, some have suggested the paradigm of a stew pot, where potatoes, carrots, meat, onions, and—I would insist!—garlic share their flavors with each other even as they remain distinct and recognizable ingredients. This is certainly a better image than the melting pot or the mosaic. All I would add is that this is a good paradigm as long as the potato has the right to classify and define itself as various circumstances require, and thus to say at times that it is a potato, at times that it is a vegetable, and at times that it is a bit of stew, without having any grand chef telling it what it should be or how it should understand itself.

In this particular context, we must be careful not to allow talk about "multiculturalism" to hide the racism that stands at the heart of the traditionally dominant culture in this nation. Indeed, I am afraid that much of the current talk about a multicultural society is a way of obscuring the racial and class issues that still divide the nation, and that will still divide it if we deal only with "cultures," forgetting the role that race and class have played and still play among us, and particularly the manner in which race has been defined in order to "justify" the existence of a permanent under-class. While the present situation makes the question of the relationship among cultures urgent, that urgency must not be allowed to eclipse the injustice suffered by many on the basis of racism, or the use of race and racism for ulterior class motives.

But back to the vision, and back to our title. If I remember my conversations with Dr. King aright, if I understand his dream correctly, if the dream is akin to the vision of John on Patmos, then there are two main points that must be made at this particular historical junction.

The first of these should be quite obvious from my earlier remarks: a truly multicultural vision is a dynamic one. The future for which we must strive out of this vision is a future where cultures and races will have the freedom to define themselves. It is a future where no one race, no one culture, will have the power to define others, to tell them their place in society, or to determine what their identity or their contribution to the whole will be. It is a future where cultures will not simply be tolerated or allowed to exist side by side, but where cultures and races will be open to each other, where our very definitions of race and culture will be up for constant redefinition, where they will not be used to classify, to exclude, or to establish distance, but to establish connections, to do justice, to provide avenues for love and for interaction.

The second point should be just as obvious, although it may be more difficult for Americans—even liberal Americans—to accept. Let me state it quite bluntly: If all we strive for is a multicultural

America, even in the sense that I have just described, then there is no future for such an America. The dream, like Dr. King's, must deal with the issues at hand, with the politics and the culture of America. But the dream, also like Dr. King's, must go beyond the borders of this nation. If it is true that as long as someone is oppressed no one can be really free, then as long as the vision is not attained for the entire world it cannot really be attained in America. If this nation follows policies that undercut freedom and democracy in other nations, our own freedom and democracy will eventually be undercut. If the rich and powerful in this country export to other nations the inequities that are no longer tolerated here, those inequities will come back to haunt us. If we are content with having the riches of the world flow to America like so many waters, and think that we can close our borders to the miseries of the world, we shall not be true to the vision, and the dream will become a nightmare of violence and terrorism.

The dream is true. The dream is irresistible. The dream will come true. The question is not, will it happen? The question is rather, as it happens, will we be found to have resisted it? Or will we be found to have been obedient to the heavenly vision?

"After this I looked, and there was a great multitude that no one could count, from every nation, from all tribes and peoples and languages. . . . They shall sit under their own vines and under their own fig trees, and no one shall make them afraid. . . . They shall beat their swords into plowshares, and their spears into pruning hooks; nation shall not lift up sword against nation, neither shall they learn war any more." We have a dream!

chapter 7

Prophesy to My People

James A. Forbes Jr.

—◁—

Dr. Martin Luther King Jr. loved the book of Amos. Oh, how many times did he say, "Let justice roll down like waters, and righteousness like a mighty stream." He loved this book. Knowing this, let us consider the prophesy of Amos (7:7-17):

> This is what he showed me: the Lord was standing beside a wall built with a plumb line, with a plumb line in his hand. And the Lord said to me, "Amos, what do you see?" And I said, "A plumb line." Then the Lord said,
> "See, I am setting a plumb line in the midst of my people Israel; I will never again pass them by.
> The high places of Isaac shall be made desolate,
>   and the sanctuaries of Israel shall be laid waste,
>   and I will rise against the house of Jeroboam with the sword."
> Then Amaziah, the priest of Bethel, sent to King Jeroboam of Israel, saying, "Amos has conspired against you in the very center of the house of Israel; the land is not able to bear all his words. For thus Amos has said,
> 'Jeroboam shall die by the sword and Israel must go into exile away from his land.'"
> And Amaziah said to Amos, "O seer, go, flee away to the land of Judah, earn your bread there, and prophesy there; but never again prophesy at Bethel, for it is the king's sanctuary, and it is a temple of the kingdom."
> Then Amos answered Amaziah, "I am no prophet, nor a prophet's son; but I am a herdsman, and a dresser of sycamore

trees, and the Lord took me from following the flock, and the
Lord said to me, 'Go, prophesy to my people Israel.'
 Now, therefore, hear the word of the Lord.
 You say, 'Do not prophesy against Israel,
  and do not preach against the house of Isaac.'
 Therefore thus says the Lord:
 'Your wife shall become a prostitute in the city,
  and your sons and your daughters shall fall by the sword,
  and your land shall be parceled out by line;
  you yourself shall die in unclean lands,
  and Israel shall surely go into exile away from its land.'"

First, let us take care that we do not hear an anti-Semitic attitude in this message from Amos. After all, it is a text from Hebrew Scripture. It is a text in which there is a word for each one of us, whatever our religious tradition or background may be.

Yes, King loved the book of Amos. But more than that, his ministry was an example of what we have read. God gave Martin Luther King Jr. a plumb line to hold up against the policies and practices of his time, even as God gave Amos a vision of a plumb line to hold up in respect to his people. So let us try to get into our heads something about this plumb line.

I need to acknowledge that I am not following here the ideal homiletic approach usually taught to students. I am simply moving as the Spirit moves me from one thing to the other, but my goal is very clear. I don't usually give my sermonic idea or my propositional statement at the beginning; I teach my students not to do that. But this is too serious a message to keep hidden: I propose to show that people of genuine and mature faith in God are given the plumb line of a prophetic perspective by which they are able to challenge and engage their leaders and fellow citizens in building up a more peaceful, just, and compassionate society.

Dr. Henry Mitchell, one of my mentors in the art of preaching and the author of *Black Preaching*, said it is not enough to tell people what you are going to say. In addition to a preacher knowing what he or she wants to say, a preacher should also know what behavioral results he or she hopes will come out of the preaching event. So here are my hopes for readers of this essay: First, that they answer the call to be conscientious believers; second, that they make a fresh commitment of time, talent, and resources in service of the call to peace, justice, and compassion; and third, that they commit to helping build a movement for the spiritual renewal and healing and empowerment of our nation, the United States of America—including the recovery of its vocation of promoting life, liberty, and the pursuit of happiness for ourselves and freedom, justice, equality, and peace for our neighbors around the world.

Now that's all I want to do. If I can get that done, I think maybe the Lord would say, "Well done, brother Jim."

But let's get started. Let's go back and say a word about plumb lines. Most of the people in my community in New York don't know anything about a plumb line. Let me describe it for you. A plumb line is a string with a small weight like a spinning top attached to the end. If you can imagine somebody laying bricks or building a wall, the builder needs a way to make sure the wall is straight and upright. If you suspend the plumb line along the wall, you are able to see if the wall is being built correctly. If a brick is out of order, you push it just a little because the plumb line will not lie about the straightness of the wall.

This is what the prophet Amos is about. Even the first sentence in his prophesy says, "This is what he showed me," because God worked with Amos with images, and the image is about a plumb line. The reality is that we who come after Dr. King need to understand that Dr. King wasn't simply telling folks what his ideas were. He believed he had been called by God to hold up a plumb line. In fact, in regards to "I Have a Dream," the issue is not just what was Dr. King's dream—the issue is where did he get the dream. See, what we have to do is get reconnected to the One that gave King his dream. And if we get reconnected with the One that gave King his dream, we can stop picking on it as *his* dream.

I want to know: What dream did the Lord give *you?* Has God given you a dream? Do you have a vision of the kind of world you want to live in? Do you have some sense of what the relationship would be between the rich and the poor, the blacks and the whites, the Latinos and Native Americans, the Afghanis and Iraqis? How would problems get solved if the world were as you wanted to see it? In fact, I want to make this case: I don't even want a dialogue with anybody who isn't willing first to sit down and say, "Listen, I have a vision of how things ought to be." Share your vision! Because clearly, if your vision and my vision are completely opposite, the prospect of our working collaboratively to achieve our goals will be very weak indeed. It is important that every religious person—Christian, Jew, Lutheran, Sikh, Buddhist, Hindu, whatever—everybody needs to have a vision of what the world looks like from a perspective of their faith, and needs to work toward the achievement of that end.

Imagine here a choir singing for us, "Open my eyes that I may see glimpses of truth thou hast for me. Place in my hands the wonderful key that shall unclasp and set me free. Silently now, I wait for thee, ready, my God, thy will to see. Open my eyes. Illumine me, Spirit divine."

Let me say more soberly, brothers and sisters, that much of the talk you hear in our nation today does not make a reference to the vision God has given. People in churches all over this land claim to be inspired by God but they make no reference to having been in contact with God. In Jeremiah, there is a critique that says, "Woe unto that prophet who is running and has seen nothing." Has God shown you a plumb line? Your values: are they simply the codification of the interests of your in-group? Are you simply using religion to sanctify what seems to be convenient to you and your crowd? Or are you really sure that you had a conversation with God about politics, about economics, about race relations, about interfaith relations with other people?

Now let us recall another prophet, Isaiah, even as we recall Amos. God, in Isaiah 58, is like a wounded, disappointed, jilted lover saying "You are supposed to be my people and yet you are always thinking about yourselves." God gets so sick and tired of our projecting our preferences into the mouth of God, playing ventriloquist. So, if you will, God made me the lawyer to speak up about all those fraudulent claims: "God told me to do this," "God told me to fight them," "God told me to destroy the others." The issue is, what has God shown us? Have we stayed in the presence of God long enough for God to give us some sense of God saying, "This I don't like. This I do like. Could you get me this? Could you support me? Help me. I have some ideas about how I want things done, but my thoughts are not your thoughts and my ways are not your ways. Listen to me. Listen to me. And remember, if you do, you will be aligned with something that is substantial, for my words will not return unto me void, but will accomplish the purpose whereunto I have sent it."

That is what happened to Amos. Amos didn't go around trying to say something that would make it appear that God was ordaining him to do it. In fact, the brother says, "I am no prophet. I am not even the son of a prophet. So I am not even doing it because I am trying to act like my daddy who went before me. I am not even in the guild of the prophets. In fact, I was taking care of my own business. I was a herdsman by trade. I was just a person who dressed the sycamore tree. And I was doing good; my business was flourishing. I would take my apples whenever they were ready. Listen, it wasn't anything I saw. It was not my time to satisfy my grandma. I was doing what I was doing and the Lord came to me and spoke to me and said, 'Amos, there's some things down in Bethel that I want straightened out. And I just don't want them to assume that they can get away with it without at least my saying something about it. So go down; go and get them. Go to Bethel, and tell them that if they are not careful things are not going to be well for them. You just go up there and tell them.' And so I just did it!" says Amos.

Let's stop right now for station identification. The question here is: Have you got a call? Whatever perspective you are promoting in the world today, did you get a call? Has God spoken to you? Has God said, "This is what I want you to do"? Or did you just play along with conformity to other things in your neighborhood, in your political party, in your ideological framework? Has God called? I am raising this question for churches as well as individuals.

The big challenge in today's world is how to respond to September 11. Everybody fell in line with the revenge ethic, running after a war on terror as if it had become the primary vocation of our nation just to build weapons and go and arm nations and round up terrorists. I know we've got to be secure. I am grateful for the work that has been done to help us be somewhat less vulnerable. And I am grateful that there is somebody who can ferret out where the danger is.

But we need to look at the truth that churches all over the United States of America opted into a psychic and emotional frenzy about getting even, getting back, making sure that the whole world knows that "We ain't taking this sitting down!" and "We're going to get you for this!" Something about that is odious to God, and there's been a complicity of silence. Christians all over the United States went into their churches and sat and were silent. It was almost as if nobody was asking God, "What's your take on this thing? And what kind of a coach would you be to our nation? How do you want your religious people to act?" But if it is possible that God was relying upon God's people in churches to stand up for what at least approximated the principles of the prophets, or the principles of the Gospel, then God must be disappointed.

Brothers and sisters, my purpose here is to say the Lord is calling congregations; the Lord is calling ministers; the Lord is calling laypeople, saying, "I have some ideas about how to make the world safe. I have some ideas about what will sustain my creation. I have some ideas about what's ugly and what's odious and how some changes will have to take place."

And just so, Amos heard a call. And when he heard a call, he said, "Yes, Lord." In my church they sing a little song that is easy to learn, but it can get hot! They sing, "Yessss, yessss, yessss, yessss, yessss, yessss, yessss." But the truth of the matter is, we ought to sing that song the other way. God says, "I want you to stand up for justice, for truth; I want you to eschew the violent spirit that is so gripping the world today; I want you to speak truth to those who are blindly following military individuals yet discover they are less safe than they were before." And when God calls us to stand up for a new principle of peace that is not based on the arrogance and pride of the number-one superpower in the world, we all too often sing, "Noooo, noooo, noooo, noooo, noooo, noooo, noooo."

I am not unaware that what I am saying is radical. I was asking my wife the other day, "Bettye, you know, I am trying to convey what God is calling us to do, and I need some help. I want to say, 'Stand up. Speak out.' If I go first with stand up and then speak out, then what's the next thing?" And she said, "Get killed." (Sometimes out of the mouths of babes, and sometimes out of the mouths of wives!) Indeed, there is a challenge. As with the call of Amos, there is a serious challenge.

To be fair, let us examine what that challenge is. If a congregation, or an individual minister, decides to say yes to God's call for radical obedience, it would be unfair for me not to say that, just as Amos was put out of Bethel, we may be met with hostility. Amaziah said, "Not here, you won't."

And the same was true for Dr. King. It's wonderful that every January we talk about "I Have a Dream." But it's almost profane to portray that speech as "exhibit A" of what his life was like. Folks, the man was hated. And before you white people get nervous—he was hated by black folks, too. The President of the National Baptist Convention, J. H. Jackson, didn't want him in his pulpit. A whole lot of folks didn't want Dr. King around. I listened to tapes where they were booing and hissing at him. When he went up to Grosse Pointe in Michigan, they could hardly complete the meeting because of the booing from the audience.

He spent more days in jail than any other preacher we know. Not because of criminality, but because he dared to say, "Yessss, yessss, yessss, yessss, yessss." He was hardly home with his family, hardly had time to raise his children. There were turncoats in the movement, people who tried to undermine the movement. Some people say, "Oh, this must have been a wonderful man." "I want to be like Mike," people said, and they were not talking about Michael Jordan. They called King "Mike," you see. They acted like that. But oh, how much rudeness he endured.

People think he must have felt God's presence with him to be able to say those wonderful words that have inspired and changed our nation. They didn't know the anguish of the spirit he suffered. Do you know the sense of foreboding that followed him, especially in those awful last days when he was in the garbage workers' strike? His colleagues said he had this dark sense of impending doom. Do you understand that anguish?

Well, that is what we are trying to grasp here. It's not fair to encourage you to say yes to the Lord without also saying that, whether it is Amos or whether it is King, there's a price that has to be paid. Are you sure you want to be a prophet? If you know what's involved in a prophetic ministry, you might want to ask the Lord, "Why don't you choose somebody else?" It takes courage.

Let's get some reality here on the actions the leaders of our country have been taking. Is it because there has been a great referendum? It was set up in Luke's Gospel: "You cannot serve God and Mammon." So since you cannot have both of them on the throne in America, a referendum has been held, and I have done some interviewing at exit polls. On the basis of an early projection, who do you think won the vote? Who won the race between God and Mammon in America? I think it is beyond question that in our nation, money translates into convenience, into honor, into opportunity. Nice house. Good job. First-rate education. That is the way it's done in America.

It is not easy to be prophetic in a time when the ranking deity is material wealth and the ultimate manifestation of power is military prowess. It takes courage to stand up and decide you are going to say yes to God, who has said that a man or a woman's life consists not in the abundance of things he or she possesses. This explains why so many of us were silent.

But Amos—I am not saying I want to be like Amos—but Amos, even when Amaziah told him to go away, did not back down. We make excuses for timidity, saying, "Well, I discharged my responsibilities." What does Amos do? Amos, after being chastised and told "Get out of here," still stands up and delivers the rest of what the Lord told him to say. I don't know why Amaziah or Jereboam did not finish him off then and there. Maybe the Lord was with him to say to him, "Not only did you speak it, but you have been a master of oratory. Now go back and get it written down so that others may learn to listen to what I say." To say the truth and then to write it down so that it is clear to all—that takes courage, congregations: courage to be faithful and fruitful.

The reason we don't do some of the things that the gospel calls us to do is because courage is a hard commodity to come by. So where do you get courage from? You know what I think? I think that part of the courage is in the call. When I teach homiletics, the first thing I ask the students to do is to tell me about their call, because if I had not been called to this ministry by God telling me what to do with my life, I am not sure but that I would have been more cowardly than I actually have been.

Every time I have been tempted to back up from the truth that God has placed in my life, I remember several things. I remember that God called me. I even remember where I was the night that I was called. I was working at the Francis Scott Key Hotel in Washington D.C. that whole week. Whenever I went up in the elevator to the seventh floor, a man would get off on another floor and turn around and say, "Young man, the Lord has a purpose for your life." I got so sick of it—every time I got on the elevator: "Young man, the Lord has a purpose for your life."

I was so glad when the end of the week came that I went over to 1015 "D" Street, where Rev. Lawson got up and preached from Isaiah, chapter 6, saying, "In the year that King Uzziah died, I saw also the Lord. He was high and lifted up, and his train filled the temple." The Reverend also went on to say that after the angels had appeared and the cherubim and all of that, Isaiah said, "Woe is me for I am undone!" And Rev. Lawson stopped and said, "Let me explain this business about being undone." He said that, in the country, children eat a lot of molasses and sometimes it is all Momma can do to keep the biscuits on the table. He said, "One morning I heard the kids saying, 'Mom, we need more biscuits.' But Mom said, 'Well, that's all right. You are just going to have to wait. The biscuits are in the oven, but they ain't done yet.'"

And he said, "There are some folks like that." Why would he say that? He explained that there's some folks like that in the oven, but they ain't done yet. And I got to thinking about myself. I had my plans as to what I wanted to do with my life and I was in the oven, but I wasn't done yet. Oh, that troubled me, that God wasn't finished with me. God hadn't made clear what I was to do with my life.

I recall so very well that I went home that night, over on Harvard Street where I lived, and put on my music. I was a highfalutin' Howard University student; I liked high-class music. So I put on Tchaikovsky's Symphony no. 4 in F Minor and thought that would calm my nerves down a little bit. And I sat there enjoying the music, that energetic opening passage. I was beginning to feel better—until it got down to the final movement. And do you know what? Eugene Ormandy and the Philadelphia Orchestra were pressed into service because I thought I heard these words, sitting there in that living room, "Jim Forbes, don't you know I have called you? Jim Forbes, don't you know I have called you? Yes, oh yes, I have called you." I said, "Oh, this can't be!" But the music was just as insistent, and I felt I couldn't back away from this experience. I said, "Oh, no. I've got to accept this ministry." And then I said, "Oh, Lord, I am so sorry, but I don't want to do this."

And yet the Lord seemed to suggest to me, "Don't worry. Just open your Bible." I opened my Bible and it turned to Psalm 27. I am talking about where courage comes from. I turned to Psalm 27 and the Lord said, "Just read it." And I read,

> The Lord is my light and my salvation;
> > whom shall I fear?
> The Lord is the stronghold of my life;
> > of whom shall I be afraid?
> When evildoers assail me to devour my flesh—
> my adversaries and foes—
> > they shall stumble and fall.
> Though an army encamp against me,
> > my heart shall not fear;
> though wars shall rise up against me,
> > yet I will be confident.

I read the whole psalm and then I was led to close the Bible.

Then the Lord said, "Now recite it." I said, "I can't because I haven't learned it." And the Lord said, "Try it now." So I started:

"The Lord is my light and my salvation; whom shall I fear? The Lord is the stronghold of my life; of whom shall I be afraid?" And all the way to the call to "be strong, and let your heart take courage; wait for the Lord!"

Having memorized the psalm so quickly, I thought that God was saying, "If you accept my call to the ministry, you are going to be blessed with phenomenal memory." But that was not the meaning of that experience. The meaning was this: if the Lord calls you, even if you don't feel like it, don't back up. It might not be easy, but press your way because God, who gives the call, gives us something to help us to stand.

In the past, when I was challenging my government, speaking about domination theory, empire building, spinning lies, the feud, gathering resources at the expense of the others, I thought, Jim, why are you so cantankerous? But now I think of my role in a different way. Now, at last, I know that I am not unpatriotic when I dare to tell the truth to my nation. I am prophetically patriotic when I challenge the evils of the growing gap between the haves and the have-nots, if I say that some people use their political power to gather resources that will enrich them and impoverish others, that some people dare to believe that they and they alone can take the destiny not only of a whole nation, but a whole globe, just to satisfy their little special interests.

Now the Lord says, "Don't feel bad, Jim. I am going to take care of you until it's time for you to die. And I am not yet telling you how you will die because you would be too sensitive waiting for how it's going to happen. So just be aware that you will be talked about. Some days you are going to be talked about like a dog." And the Lord says, "But don't, don't, don't give up on your call. What you say could be the good news the world needs to hear."

You've heard that a dog is man's best friend? Imagine that a house is on fire and the fire is in a remote room. The owner of the dog is lying fast asleep on the bed and the dog comes up—this is canine theology—and first of all, barks. You see, that's prophetic ministry barking. He barks because something is wrong. I smell smoke somewhere, he's saying. Woof! Woof! And the owner pushes the dog away. But the dog comes back anyhow. And then the dog starts pulling on the covers. Get out of here! says the owner, and pulls the covers back up. And if nothing happens, the dog starts licking the master's face. And then the master wakes up and smells the smoke and runs and calls the fire station and saves the house.

In the United States of America, I smell smoke. And the Lord is calling me to speak out, to be a barking dog. They won't like it. But for love of the nation, I will do it if it's the last barking I do. We need to pull the covers off the mendacity and lies. We need to lick the faces of oppressors even if we get slapped, because the Lord calls us to do it. The Lord will stop at nothing. God will do this to you: warn you and wake you up and finally save you.

I have been so blessed by the Lord, and so have we all. We live in a world that gives us global responsibility. People all around the world—Iraqis, Pakistanis, Muslims, Jews, Sikhs, Africans, Asians, Pacific Islanders—look to us. They are all God's children. They would like to know if there is a word from the Lord. What has God said to us about how to treat them?

> I looked around the other day and saw
> How truly blessed this life of mine has been.
> I have health, strength and comforts,
> Peace and joy within;
>
> Special care in time of desperation,
> A helping hand when friends are few.
> So I asked the Lord, what can I do
> To turn some thanks to you?
>
> I expected mission impossible,
> A call to service far away.
> But instead, this gentle assignment
> God sends to me each day:

Love my children, that's all I ask of you.
Love my children, it's the least that you can do.
If you love them as I love them,
We shall see them safely through.

Love yourself, love me, too,
And whatever else you do,
Love my children.

Notes

—•—

1. King's Vision of America: An Ethical Assessment

1. The complete text of King's speech is in James Melvin Washington, ed., *A Testament of Hope: The Essential Writings of Martin Luther King, Jr.* (San Francisco: Harper & Row, 1986), 217–20.

2. The Poor People's Campaign of 1968

1. Edgar Allan Poe, *The Raven and Other Poems and Tales* (Boston: Little, Brown, 1975), 41.

2. For explanations on King's move toward the "poor," see Martin Luther King Jr., "The President's Address," given August 16, 1967, to the Tenth Anniversary Convention of the Southern Christian Leadership Conference, Atlanta, Georgia, in Robert L. Scott and Wayne Brockriede, eds., *The Rhetoric of Black Power* (New York: Harper & Row, 1969), 156.

3. King's speech is found in James Melvin Washington, ed., *A Testament of Hope: The Essential Writings of Martin Luther King, Jr.* (San Francisco: Harper & Row, 1986), 217–20.

4. From King's "Nobel Prize Acceptance Speech," found in Washington, ed., *A Testament of Hope* 224–26.

5. King's "Beyond Vietnam" speech is entitled "A Time to Break Silence" in Washington, ed., *A Testament of Hope*, 243.

6. David J. Garrow, *Bearing the Cross: Martin Luther King, Jr., and the Southern Christian Leadership Conference* (New York: Vintage, 1986), 539–40.

7. Southern Christian Leadership Conference, "Statement by Dr. Martin Luther King, Jr., President," December 4, 1967, King

Archives, Box 178, File 33; *New York Times*, December 5, 1967, 1, 32.

8. Dr. Martin Luther King, *Look*, April 16, 1968.

9. Robert T. Chase, "Class Resurrection: The Poor People's Campaign of 1968 and Resurrection City," *Essays in History* 40 (1998): 5.

10. *The Washingtonian*, February, 1968, 53.

11. See Chase, "Class Resurrection," 5, for more details about the SCLC's expanding concerns about cross-racial poverty.

12. Gerald D. McKnight, *The Last Crusade: Martin Luther King, Jr., the FBI, and the Poor People's Campaign* (Boulder: Westview, 1998), 34.

13. See Chase, "Class Resurrection," 1.

14. *Washington Post*, April 23, 1968.

3. From Prophetic Preaching to Utopian Community

1. Mircea Eliade cited in Lawrence W. Levine, *Black Culture and Black Consciousness: Afro-American Folk Thought from Slavery to Freedom* (New York: Oxford University Press, 1977).

2. Walter Brueggemann, *The Prophetic Imagination*, 2nd ed. (Minneapolis: Fortress Press, 2001), 4.

3. Martin Luther King Jr., "Letter from a Birmingham Jail," in *Why We Can't Wait* (New York: Harper & Row, 1964), 91.

4. William A. Galston, *Justice and the Human Good* (Chicago: University of Chicago Press, 1980).

5. Martin Luther King Jr., Seventh Annual Gandhi Memorial Lecture (Howard University, Washington D.C., November 6, 1966).

4. Growing like Topsy: Solidarity in a Multicultural U.S.A.

1. Harriet Beecher Stowe, *Uncle Tom's Cabin; or Life among the Lowly* (New York: A. L. Burt, 1852), 250–51. Stowe brought the abolitionists' message to the public conscience. She attempted to make whites in the South and North see slaves as human beings.

Eliza Harris, a slave whose son is to be sold, escapes her beloved home on Shelby plantation in Kentucky and heads north, eluding the hired slave catchers by using the Underground Railroad. Another slave, Uncle Tom, is sent "down the river" for sale, and ultimately endures a martyr's death under the whips of Simon Legree's overseers. *Uncle Tom's Cabin* paints pictures of three plantations, each worse than the last, where even the best plantation leaves a slave at the mercy of fate or debt.

2. Donella H. Meadows, "State of the Global Village Report," *The Global Citizen* syndicated column (May 31, 1990), available online: http://www.tidepool.org/gc/gc5.31.90.cfm.

3. Stowe, *Uncle Tom's Cabin*, 254–55. The scene ends: "St. Clare was leaning over the back of her chair. 'You find virgin soil there, Cousin; put in your own ideas, —you won't find many to pull up.'" In two places in this conversation, Jane, a maid in the household, interjects information about slave life. The first is after Topsy says she was never born: "The child was evidently sincere, and Jane, breaking into a short laugh, said, 'Laws, Missis, there's heaps of 'em. Speculators buys 'em up cheap, when they's little, and gets 'em raised for market.'" The second is after Topsy tells Miss Ophelia that she does not know how long she lived with her previous owners: "'Laws, Missis, those low negroes,—they can't tell; they don't know anything about time,' said Jane; 'they don't know what a year is; they don't know their own ages.'"

4. Katie Geneva Cannon discusses this in greater detail in her lecture, "Remembering What We Never Knew: The Epistemology of Womanist Ethics" (paper presented at the "Soul to Soul: Women and Religion in the 21st Century" conference sponsored by the Center for Women and Religion, Graduate Theological Union, Berkeley, California, February 27, 1998). James Melvin Washington discusses social amnesia in the Introduction to his edited volume *Conversations with God: Two Centuries of Prayers by African Americans* (New York: HarperPerennial Library, 1995), xxvii–xlii. Washington goes on to note that "there are grave consequences when we cannot locate and integrate the memories of our forebears," for this can lead to soul murder (xxxvii). For Washington,

we must look at the public and collective rage at injustice through an analytical procedure he calls historical demonology. This methodology assumes that demons are intelligent but thrive best when not exposed. Hence historical demonology unmasks the demons in our midst and names them with precision and clarity.

5. June Jordan, "Of Those So Close beside Me, Which Are You?" in *Technical Difficulties: African-American Notes on the State of the Union* (New York: Pantheon, 1992), 29.

6. Ralph Ellison cited in Jordan, "Of Those So Close beside Me," 28.

7. *Wall Street Journal* editorial, November 1, 2001.

5. Keeping the Dream Alive

1. See Randall N. Robinson, *The Debt: What America Owes to Blacks* (New York: Plume, 2001).

2. In June 2003, the United States Supreme Court voted on whether the University of Michigan could use race as a factor in the consideration of student applicants. See the June 23, 2003, edition of *University of Michigan News Service* for a detailed explanation and discussion of the Court's impact.

3. Martin Luther King Jr., "Non-violence and Racial Justice," *Christian Century* (February 6, 1957).

4. Martin Luther King Jr., *Where Do We Go from Here: Chaos or Community?* (Boston: Beacon, 1968), 36.

5. Quoted in David Garrow, *Bearing the Cross: Martin Luther King, Jr., and the Southern Christian Leadership Council* (New York: Vintage, 1988), 555. Also see Martin Luther King Jr., "The Drum Major Instinct," in James M. Washington, ed., *A Testament of Hope: The Essential Writings of Martin Luther King, Jr.* (San Francisco: Harper & Row, 1986), 266–67.

6. Martin Luther King Jr., "Speech at Staff Retreat Penn Center, Frogmore, South Carolina, May 23–31, 1967," 7 (author's copy).

7. Ibid., 30.

8. Ibid., 4.

9. Martin Luther King Jr., *The Trumpet of Conscience* (New York: Harper & Row, 1967), 25.

10. See "The President's Address to the Tenth Anniversary Convention of the Southern Christian Leadership Conference, Atlanta, Georgia, August 16, 1967," in Robert L. Scott and Wayne Brockriede, eds., *The Rhetoric of Black Power* (New York: Harper & Row, 1969), 155.

11. Ibid., 162, 163.

12. King, *The Trumpet of Conscience*, 24. King reiterates this point on page 4 of his "A Proper Sense of Priorities" speech to Clergy and Laity Concerned about Vietnam, at New York Avenue Presbyterian Church, Washington D.C., February 2, 1968; text found at the Martin Luther King, Jr. Center in Atlanta, Georgia. Similarly, we find these words in his "A Time to Break Silence," in Washington, ed., *A Testament of Hope*, 233.

13. Quoted in James H. Cone, *Martin & Malcolm & America: A Dream or a Nightmare?* (Maryknoll, N.Y.: Orbis, 1991), 240.

14. King, *The Trumpet of Conscience*, 62.

15. Martin Luther King Jr., "Beyond Vietnam" (New York: Clergy and Laity Concerned, 1982), 9.

16. King, *The Trumpet of Conscience*, 62.

17. Ibid., 49–50.

18. King, "A Testament of Hope," *Playboy* (January 1969), reprint, 4.

19. Martin Luther King Jr., "A Time to Break Silence," in Washington, ed., *A Testament of Hope*, 234.

6. The Dream

1. Justo González, *For the Healing of the Nations: The Book of Revelation in an Age of Cultural Conflict* (Maryknoll, N.Y.: Orbis, 1999).

2. The person denied the right to serve as a witness was Manuel Domínguez, who had served as a delegate to the California State Constitutional Convention in 1849. In 1857, he was barred from serving as a witness because, as a Mexican, he was an Indian. The

story is told in Tomás Almaguer, *Racial Faultlines: The Historical Origins of White Supremacy in California* (Berkeley: University of California Press, 1994), 57. It is discussed, along with its implications, by Teresa Chávez Sauceda, in "Race, Religion and La Raza," in David Maldonado Jr., ed., *Protestantes/Protestants: Hispanic Christianity within Mainline Traditions* (Nashville: Abingdon, 1999), 178.